JOURNEY INTO THE UNKNOWN

JOURNEY INTO THE UNKNOWN

Bridget Teresa Dunne

TEMPLE PUBLISHING COMPANY
LONDON, ENGLAND

First published in 1992
by Vantage Press, USA
Revised edition published in Great Britain 1995
by Temple Publishing Company
London, England

Copyright © Bridget Teresa Dunne 1992, 1995

British Library Cataloguing-in-Publication Data.
A catalogue record for this book is available
from the British Library

ISBN 1 85977 095 9

All rights reserved. No part of this publication
may be reproduced, stored in a retrieval system or
transmitted in any form or by any means, electronic,
mechanical, photocopying, recording or otherwise,
without the prior permission of the publisher.

The right of Bridget Teresa Dunne to be identified
as the author of this work has been asserted by
her in accordance with the Copyright, Designs
and Patents Act 1988.

Cover design by Harold King

Printed & bound in England by
Antony Rowe Ltd, Chippenham, Wiltshire

To my children,
Katrina Maria and Mark John

Contents

Foreword	ix
Chapter One	1
Two	7
Three	25
Four	47
Five	51
Six	57
Seven	61
Eight	67
Nine	73
Ten	79
Eleven	93

FOREWORD

I first met the author, Bridget Teresa Dunne, in the early 1940s when she was a young student nurse at the Royal Hospital, Putney, London, and I was the sister tutor. Even at that early stage, she could express herself so clearly in the test papers I set.

I was not in the least surprised when I read her moving story, *Journey into the Unknown*, especially the chapter when she bade good-bye to her darling mother on that small Kingscourt station, not knowing when or how she would ever see her again. She said she wept her eyes out. When I read her manuscript I wept, too.

I am positive it will go far, because it was written from the heart of this sensitive author. I wish her all the success in the world.

A. Mary Smitheram

1

It was the sixth of September 1939, and Germany and Britain were at war. I stood with my mother on a small railway station in Kingscourt, County Cavan, Ireland. I was just seventeen and leaving home for the first time.

My destination that day was Dublin City, which I had never before visited. My final destination, however, was a convent in Kent, where I was to study the French language, before going on again to the motherhouse in Nevers, France, and, I hoped, becoming a nun.

My mother had arranged a short holiday for me in Dublin, feeling uneasy about me being so young and going to England where there was a war. I was going to be met by and stay with two reputable Catholic ladies who ran a guest house in Clontarf, County Dublin. My mother, in her wisdom, knew how I felt, and said should I change my mind, I could always return, as Dublin was only fifty miles away.

The week before I left, I had been in a constant state of excitement and apprehension. Joining a convent had always been something important I wanted to do, but I was worried about the coming separation and leaving my mother and going to a country that was at war.

My mother was a midwife by profession (not registered) and had been a widow for ten years. My father died at the age of forty when I was seven, in 1929, from rheumatic heart disease. He was a craftsman thatcher, and no doubt his early death could be attributed to the many drenchings he got through the nature of his job. I do not recall him very clearly, because he spent more time in hospital than at home.

Mother was a truly remarkable lady. She was equally at home delivering a newborn baby or laying out the dead or planting a garden of potatoes. Her ethical, moral and religious beliefs were so high (and her example so compelling) they have remained with me throughout my life. I never heard her swear or say anything bad about anyone. In the week before my departure, all of us gathered each night round the hearth to recite the family rosary, and Mother led us in the meditations on each mystery.

That week, too, my thoughts were filled with Hazel, a lifelong school friend to whom, only two months before, I had bade goodbye forever. She had entered the Poor Clares, from where you were never allowed home except for the death of a parent. I did not realise how Hazel's decision had affected mine until the week before I too was due to leave home. My mother, who had a cousin who was a nun in America, did not try to dissuade me. She went along with my decision and left the rest to God and prayer.

The days before my departure I hardly slept at all, worrying about going and the moment I would walk out of the door and say goodbye to my sisters and brothers. My mother and I discussed this and decided it was best not to tell them I was going, as this might make it more difficult for the girl who was to mind them until my mother got home. We decided to say I was going to Kingscourt to get provisions, a deception that made it much harder for me to play with my sister and baby brother in that last anxious week! During our last playtime, I had to hide my tears from them. I told them something had caught in my throat, and they believed me. That last playtime was painful. I had to keep turning away, and the tears burnt my eyes like salt. The last night, when I tucked them up in bed, I really broke down as I kissed them goodnight. Neither my mother nor I slept all night. We were both in the kitchen making tea at 3 a.m. Then we both went back to bed for an hour and slept fitfully.

The morning of departure came suddenly. I was devastated at the very thought of saying goodbye, but that may have been because my lack of sleep over the past week had caught up with me. I was glad I could wash outside in a

CHAPTER ONE

tin basin, because as I did so, I had to keep wiping the flowing tears from my face. My eyes were red and burning. My darling mother made me eat her last fresh egg, though it nearly choked me, saying, 'You must eat, Bridget, because it is a long journey to Kingscourt, and the walk will make you hungry.' At last, the moment of kissing my sisters and brothers goodbye came. I felt sick, but tried to hide it from them so as not to make it more difficult for my mother when I had gone. I merely said, 'Bye, bye, Teresa and Peter.'

At last, we were on the three mile trek to the station, a lonely road where at times you never even saw a donkey or cart on the way. I was pleased that day not to have met a neighbour. As soon as we reached the main road we recited the rosary. I was sobbing, and I could sense my mother was really brokenhearted, because in between the decades, I heard many a sigh and sob, which she, in her great wisdom, tried to hide from me. Once she rubbed her eyes with a hankie, telling me she thought a fly had got into her eyes, but I knew differently because, she being a nurse, would have stopped and asked me to remove the fly with the corner of her hankie. Instead, she kept saying, 'Have you got your rosary beads, Bridget? Promise me you will always try and say one decade of the rosary each day.' I promised I would, for, after all, Our Lady pleaded with St Bernadette of Lourdes to say the rosary for the conversion of Russia.

We reached the station. My mother bought a single ticket to Dublin for me and we went onto the platform to wait for the train. A train was coming as we arrived, and that threw me into a panic. I said, 'There's one coming, Mother. Is it the Dublin train?'

'No, Daughter,' she replied. 'Yours is not due for ten minutes. The guard said so. Come and sit down.'

As I sat down and snuggled up to my mother I wished it were all a bad dream. I was dressed that morning in my nappa blue coat and hat, which was part of my new convent school uniform. In fact, it was the first new article of clothing I had ever had. I (tightly) held a small cardboard suitcase in my hand. It contained all my bits. I was shaking and powerless to control myself.

Then suddenly I heard a train in the distance and was again panic-stricken. I almost shouted at my mother, 'Is this mine?' Even though it was forty-four years ago, I shall never forget the lonesome look on her face then, as she tried to hide her tears. The train pulled in and people opened the doors and I too boarded it. My mother pushed her last ten shillings into my hand saying, 'Daughter, never be afraid of your religion or heritage; these can never be taken from you.' I knew it was her last note, and I cried bitterly.

Then the doors closed, and the train pulled out so quickly I could barely see the back of my mother and her frantically waving and rubbing her red eyes. I drenched the only hankie I had, and the tears once again burnt my eyes like salt.

I found a seat and sat down full of panic and sobbing out loud, so much so that my whole body was shaking and I was powerless to control myself. Then suddenly I felt a warm arm on my shoulder and heard someone saying, 'Why are you so upset dear? Are you leaving home for the first time?' I nodded. 'I fully understand,' the voice went on. 'I felt just like you twenty years ago when I said goodbye to my mother on this same station.'

I looked up and saw the face of a lovely nun who had first taught me when I was a child at my first school. 'You have no need to fear. You were bright. Just snuggle up to me and treat me as a mother.' She wanted to know how I got on at school and where was I going that day? I told her my plans and what I hoped to do in the future, but said I was going to Dublin that day. I felt more comfortable with the sister, but still I sobbed all the way to Dublin, worrying about my mother.

It had been arranged previously that I should spend a week in Dublin with two ladies who had a guest house outside the city. They were meeting me at Amien Street station, Dublin, and I was going to board with them for a week before leaving to meet my teacher and fellow students at Dun Laoghaire docks. I have always been grateful to my mother for the first holiday I ever had. She knew well how I felt and thought it would help to relax and prepare me for the new life that lay ahead of me in England.

CHAPTER ONE

As my train steamed into Dublin, I was panic-stricken, wondering what I should do if I missed the two ladies! Thankfully, I spotted them waving two red scarves to attract my attention. The lovely sister who had comforted me on the journey put her arm around me, saying, 'Now, my dear, I'm sure these lovely ladies will take good care of you. God bless you and every happiness for your new life ahead.'

I tearfully said, 'Thanks a lot. I shall always remember you in my prayers and Holy Communion.'

The ladies approached me, gently saying, 'You must be Bridget,' then they hugged me tenderly.

'My little dear,' said one, 'you have been crying. Dry your eyes. You will be happy with us. During the week we will show you around Dublin City and point out to you all the interesting places, which I'm sure you have read about in your school books.' As I stood there and looked around I was mesmerised at this station and what I could see of the great city.

We boarded a city bus for our short journey to Clontarf. On the way out they noticed how drenched my hankie was. Madge, the younger one, took out two beautiful white handkerchiefs and handed them to me, saying, 'Use these and don't be afraid. We can soon wash and boil them for you.'

At last, we reached their lovely white house in Clontarf. All during the way they kept pointing out to me the interesting places, but I was so excited I could not take it all in. As we walked up the avenue to the house I could see pretty tubs of mixed flowers on each side of the door. Their scent was powerful from the night-scented stock. We went in, and at once I felt at home, seeing the turf fire in the open grate. For tea we had my favourite, a fresh-boiled egg, brown bread and butter and homemade cakes. As I ate, I could not help wondering how my mother could pay my board, which at that time was thirty shillings for the week.

I was their sole guest that week, and each day after breakfast they were delighted to show me around Dublin City to visit the numerous churches and cathedrals. I stood in awe and wonder that man could build such beautiful places for us to enjoy and pray in. We spent most of one day in Phoenix Park, where the late Eamon De Valera and his wife had lived! Their house was shaded by high trees, and there were acres of gardens. On the Thursday we went to Trinity College, where I saw for the first time the famous *Book of Kells* displayed in a glass case. Even though we spent three hours there, I did not want to come away. There were so many interesting things to see. We went from Trinity to the Pro-cathedral Dublin, where that day there happened to be a society wedding. My eyes nearly dropped out of my head at the grandeur. The stained-glass window over the high altar reminded me of childhood rainbows.

Towards the end of the week, I had a letter from my mother, and enclosed was the thirty shillings for my board, which I duly handed over. However, the kind ladies told me to write to my mother and send it back, saying, 'The lady who occupied your bed last week paid for you.' To this day, I never found out who this lady was. Still, I never forget to pray for her. Needless to say, my mother was delighted, because that money bought the groceries for two weeks for all three of them.

On third of October 1939, I was taken to Dun Laoghaire docks to meet our French teacher and fellow students. We were booked on the 9 pm boat for Holyhead and train for London. When we reached the docks, again, I cried my eyes out as I said good-bye to the kind ladies who had looked after me for the week. Thankfully, I now had four hankies instead of one.

2

On the fourteenth of September 1939, I set off with my teacher and fellow students for the convent at Tonbridge, to spend one year mastering the French language.

It was wartime, and London was a complete blackout except for the odd policeman carrying a tiny torch. Every time the siren sounded, we Irish girls were petrified, because we had never heard a siren before except from the fire or ambulance service. We had to cross over by tube to get our train for Tonbridge from Charing Cross. In a mad rush we were falling over bodies covered in blankets and old reefer coats. I was so naïve, I thought they had been killed by German bombs. I wept bitterly until our teacher reassured us they were only sleeping.

On our train journey from Charing Cross, even though I was scared and weary, I counted every station until I saw Tonbridge. Once there we quickly picked up all our belongings and awaited our teacher's instructions. She told us the convent was sending a taxi to pick us up, but we might have to wait a bit. Though my stomach was filled with butterflies, I was longing to get the ordeal over with. Ten minutes later, the taxi arrived and we all piled in for the ten-minute journey to the convent. It was so comfortable, I wished the trip could have been longer.

At last we were there, and again I had the flutters inside me, wondering who should meet us first and when we would meet the Reverend Mother. Our teacher rang the bell and a lovely young novice welcomed us, kissing us on both cheeks saying, 'You're welcome and I'm sure you'll be very happy here.' She showed us into the parlour, which was a large plain room with a round table in the centre and chairs around the sides.

Soon we were greeted by the Reverend Mother, who was small and saintly-looking, wearing the habit of Saint Bernadette of Lourdes. She greeted us saying, 'You must be cold and hungry. I'll get Sister to show you to your dormitory, and after a quick wash, she will take you to the refectory for a hot meal.'

Soon we were sitting down enjoying the first meal since we left Dublin, and best of all, we were allowed to chat to one another about our home, schools and family.

After the meal we were shown to the chapel, where we said our night prayers. It was 7 pm and because of our long, tiring journey we were allowed to go to bed early, that night being our first. There were four beds in the dormitory, and each bed was curtained off for privacy. I was so tired I just said goodnight and fell asleep as soon as my head touched the pillow.

At 6.30 the following morning, we were awakened by a bell ringing and a young novice in a white veil singing the Hail Mary in Latin (*Ave Maria*). She told us to wash and dress in silence and she would come back to take us to the chapel for divine office, followed by Holy Mass.

After breakfast that first morning we were introduced to our French sister, Marie Theresa. She was sweet and motherly, putting us at our ease straight away saying, 'Do not worry, children; everything will be all right.' For the first time since I left home I felt at ease inside myself.

Later that same morning, Sister Marie together with another sister took us into Tonbridge to be fitted for gas masks. As soon as the mask was put on I had the jitters again and felt as if I were suffocating. Inwardly I felt I had made the wrong decision to come to a country where the Germans were dropping bombs day and night. Then we were taken to another office to get our identity cards and ration books, which we had to carry for the duration of the war. On the way home Sister told us that after lunch that day we would have our first French lesson. I had mixed emotions about

CHAPTER TWO

that, though I was happy to start learning a new language again.

In the refectory we students had a separate table from the community. During the meal silence was always observed and a sister read a chapter from Holy Scripture in English for our benefit. During the day we had two periods of recreation when we could talk to one another and do some reading, sewing, and embroidery. On special feast days, however, we were allowed to talk all day, as well as having treats in the food line. Needless to say, I loved feast days.

After a few days I settled down and came to like the peace and quiet of the community life. I particularly liked the silence and meditation, when I always felt very close to God and could listen to him and hoped he was listening to me. I loved the French language, and in many ways found it easier than the Gaelic I had had to master from the age of five at my convent school. Sister Marie used to take us for our French lesson along the lovely river Medway, which ran along near the convent.

For two months I was happier than ever I'd been in my whole life, and I used to pray that it would never end. Of course, I knew that was not possible and soon I would have to face reality. I wrote to and heard frequently from my darling mother, and sometimes when I felt down, especially at period time, I naturally longed to see her lovely face and feel her warm arms around me. Yet in my heart I knew that was not possible, because unlike school, we were never allowed to go home again unless our parents were seriously ill or dying. I loved my mother so much that was the last thing I wanted.

One day during our first month there, I, together with my fellow students, was summoned to the parlour for a pep talk with Reverend Mother, who was eighty-four at that time. I panicked again, thinking I'd done something wrong and would have to leave. But no, it was nothing like that, just a friendly chat telling us about her life in the order and how she was a postulant with Saint Bernadette of Lourdes. I was so intrigued and would have loved to know much more about what sort of a girl Bernadette was, but I was too nervous to ask questions like that. Reverend Mother told us how much Bernadette had suffered with her tuberculosis of the knee, but she insisted on carrying on scrubbing floors, even though she experienced great pain most of the time. That night in bed, when I said my prayers, I had my first real doubt as to whether I could make the grade.

Towards mid-December, my happiness came to an abrupt end. After Mass and breakfast, without any pain or previous symptoms, I suddenly vomited a large quantity of blood. This happened after cleaning my teeth. I thought to myself it was far too much to have come from my gums. I was whisked off to bed immediately while we awaited the doctor, but before he arrived I vomited again, and this sample was saved for his examination.

Strangely enough, I did not feel ill or afraid. I did worry, however, that I might not be able to continue my studies or go to France with my friends. The doctor was both worried and puzzled and could not understand how I was conscious and felt no pain. He instructed the sister, who was a trained nurse, to keep me flat and make sure no food went into my mouth until the ambulance he had summoned arrived and took me to the Kent and Sussex Hospital in Tunbridge Wells.

As soon as I arrived at the hospital, the consultant took one look at me and immediately started giving me blood intravenously, about four pints altogether. I was barrier-nursed (in a single room by a gowned, masked and gloved nurse) flat and was only allowed cool, bland fluids by mouth. The hardest thing of all for me was to try to use a bedpan lying flat, and I had a terrible fear that I would wet the bed. During that first day there, I had all sorts of doubts and fears, wondering if God was trying to tell me that, after all, I was not cut out for the many disciplines, such as the three vows – poverty, chastity, and obedience. I began to feel myself becoming angry, questioning why God had allowed me to come this far and now left me at a complete standstill.

The consultant to whom I was assigned thought the blood came from the lungs and that I must be in the late stages of tuberculosis, which was prevalent in 1939. He could not be sure, of course, until all the results of the

CHAPTER TWO

numerous tests were complete. I myself had different ideas, even though I was only seventeen.

A telegram was sent to my mother in Ireland saying I was very seriously ill and the prognosis was very poor. My poor mother, who herself was a trained nurse, sent a telegram back, asking, if it was possible, could I be returned home, even if it were by ambulance? They replied saying that was not possible, as I was much too weak and ill to travel and I needed constant supervision and nursing day and night. I myself was not worried, but under the sheets I cried bitterly, wondering how my mother, with two children, was coping with the sudden bad news. In my innocence of youth, I pleaded with God to help Mother in this crisis.

I spent my first Christmas away from home in a hospital in England, and even though I was lying flat, I had the best Christmas I can ever remember. Both the medical and domestic staff did everything possible to make us happy. On Christmas Eve, we had the staff carols in the ward, and in the dim light I thoroughly enjoyed seeing the faces of the lovely young nurses and doctors singing at the top of their voices. Afterwards, we all had hot sweet mince pies, which I'd never had before, and a drink of our choice. As I'd never tasted alcohol before, I did not know what to ask for. In the end I had my first taste of sherry. I was so naïve, I thought mince was always mince beef. My only regret was not having my darling mother with me that memorable night.

On Christmas morning the Catholic priest brought Holy Communion to the four Catholics in our ward. Santa had left me a large box of sweets. Needless to say, I was not allowed any sweets then, but I put them in my locker, hopefully to eat at a later date. Somehow, for reasons I cannot explain, I felt tons better, and I could only attribute this feeling of well-being to having received the body of Christ in Holy Communion.

On Christmas afternoon, I had a lovely surprise. Reverend Mother and Sister Marie Theresa, our French teacher, came up the ward all smiles, and carrying a Christmas present for me, also the first Christmas card I ever received in my life. At home we never could afford to send cards; neither did we receive any. That made this card very special, and to this day that card is locked away with my very special possessions. The present was a lovely blue pair of slippers, the worn remains of which I intend to keep always. They were the first pair of slippers I ever had, likewise the first Christmas present. Reverend Mother and Sister were allowed to have a little private tea with me consisting of a tasty slice of Christmas cake. Small wonder my first Christmas in England was, for me, a truly happy one.

In January 1940, after a further lot of extensive X-rays, blood tests, barium meals, enemas and sputum tests, they could not find out where the massive haemorrhage came from or, more importantly, what I was suffering from. The top consultant from Guy's Hospital was puzzled and admitted he had never before come across a case like mine, furthermore, as I had lost nearly all the blood from my body, it was a miracle that I lived through it. The notes he wrote on my medical record were as follows: 'We'll discharge this case as cured, but there is always the possibility that it can occur at a future date.' I was discharged to an observation wing of a sanatorium in Kent, where instinctively I kept right away from anyone whom I thought to be infectious, because I always dreaded tuberculosis.

In the observation wing of the sanatorium I became friendly with a young girl called Primrose, who took me under her wing. That first night we talked for hours about our schools and families. She was also a convent school girl and my age. They had discovered Primrose had a shadow on her lung, which was now healed, and she was ready for discharge in two weeks' time. It was during my stay there that Primrose and I decided on a nursing career. We told the doctors and nurses about our thoughts, and they helped us to fill in the application forms to train at the Ashford hospital for two years. If we were successful in two years we could be the proud owners of the prized Tuberculosis Association certificate. I discussed this with Reverend Mother, who thought it was a splendid idea, saying, 'You can spend your days off here and always treat the convent as your home.' I was delighted, thanking God.

In March 1940, following a successful interview, I started

CHAPTER TWO

my two-year training with Primrose at Ashford Sanatorium, where we both loved every minute of our brand new life. I spent my days off between the convent and Primrose's house, and life was exciting and wonderful. We both worked hard both on the ward and at our studies, and we each received a salary of thirty shillings a month. As I had never had any money in my life, this, to me, was great. Often I was able to send my dear mother ten shillings a month home, never forgetting that she gave me her last ten shillings the day I bade her goodbye at Kingscourt rail station.

Following our two years' study there, Primrose and I sat our final examination for the tuberculosis certificate and passed with flying colours. This meant we could now apply to a general hospital to study for state registration in two years instead of three and a half years.

In 1942, Primrose and I applied to take our general training at the Kent and Sussex Hospital, Tunbridge Wells, and were accepted to start in the next class in May of 1942. Meantime, I just saved enough money for my fare home to see once again my darling mother and Teresa and Peter. The war here was still raging, especially when the Germans started sending their manless planes, known by the name of Doodlebugs. In the two years since I left home I never knew what it was to sleep undisturbed in my room, either at the convent or at the hospital; needless to say, I was longing for my own little humble tick bed, which I shared with my sister Teresa. As Ireland was neutral, I longed to be able to go to bed and not have to get up when the sirens sounded. Sometimes, too, I had to do firewatching duty at the hospital.

At last, the great day arrived, and all excited, I travelled by train to Holyhead in North Wales to catch the mail boat to the Dun Laoghaire docks. It was a frightfully slow journey across the Irish Sea on what was no better than a cattle boat, where we were herded like animals for the market. As soon as we reached Dun Laoghaire I cried for joy to see once more the bright lights of Dublin City and no blackout in sight. To me it felt like heaven on earth. I caught a train into Westland Row station, where I enjoyed a lovely cooked breakfast – bacon, egg – the lot for about five shillings.

I spent all day in Dublin, because there was only one bus to take me to near my home in the country. Finally I reached the head of the lane leading to our house, and in the distance I caught a glimpse of my darling mother holding Teresa and Peter by the hand. Mother let go and soon they both were entwined in my arms. I shall always remember the smile on Mother's face as she said, 'Thank God you're here at last. I never thought I should see you again.'

After two weeks of bliss, it was time to return to England to start my general training at the Kent and Sussex Hospital. I dreaded the parting from my mother and family again. I had not slept properly for the last two nights at home but kept quiet so as not to worry my mother or wake Teresa and Peter.

Yet in some ways I was looking forward to meeting up with Primrose again and getting started on work and study, which we both found much more tiring and demanding than the tuberculosis training. It was a top teaching hospital so the rules were strict, but having been taught by nuns helped us to accept it. For instance, we had to be in our rooms by 10 pm, when the home sister who acted as our mother did a round of all the bedrooms each night. (What a change in the discipline today from the average nineteen-year-olds where parents do not know half the time where their youngsters are or whom they are with. I'm glad I knew exactly where I could go and, more importantly, how far!).

At the end of two years both Primrose and I passed our state finals with flying colours and were proud to win the lovely silver and blue badges with our numbers on their register on the back. Following three months' staffing, we moved on to the capital, where we specialised in fevers and tropical medicine. Here we really met with and treated every type of infectious disease; for instance, poliomyelitis, and sadly, tubercular meningitis, where young men and women lived for just three weeks and faded away like skeletons before death. There was no cure then for tubercular meningitis. Little children died from both diphtheria and whooping cough. Primrose and I qualified for that certificate in one year. From there we moved to Leeds Medical School, attached to a maternity hospital, where we studied midwifery for six months, after which we obtained the certificate for part one midwifery. This enabled us, if we wished, to study at Leeds University for the Royal Sanitary Examination for a health visitor. This great opportunity we availed ourselves of while we were there, and we qualified.

April 1943, I started my general training at the Kent and Sussex Hospital, Tunbridge Wells, for state registration. As I was already trained in tuberculosis, I started as a second-year student nurse. I found this very hard, being a second-year student again. It meant I was at the beck and call of the staff nurses and sisters, many of whom treated you like dirt. It took me weeks to get used to nursing on an acute medical ward where many young patients were dying with chronic nephritis. There were no dialysis units then, neither were there any kidney transplants, so, sadly, many young people died from kidney failure.

One of my jobs as a second-year student was to spend whole mornings in the sluice room testing urine. I hated that job, because the results were always the same at the end of the day and the patients always died. During my three months on that ward I became very attached to a lady in her thirties who was terminally ill and knew it. I could not bear to think that one day when I reported for duty she would not be there. One day she gave me a lovely snap of herself taken on board ship while on a cruise. I have still got that snap today, and every time I look at it I'm as near to tears as the day she died.

At the end of three months I got a good report and moved to a children's ward where many of them were suffering from coeliac disease, which rendered them unable to digest proteins, and they had have to have a gluten-free diet. Essentially, they should have had lots of fresh bananas, but because of the war we were unable to import them, so these little children had to make do with dried bananas. A feature of this disease was a pot-bellied condition with clay-coloured stools. Sadly, too, many of these little ones died young. On that ward, too, there were many lovely-looking children born with spina bifida. They were paralysed from the waist downwards and rarely lived beyond fourteen years.

Thankfully, today these children can be operated on and their severed spines connected, leading to a perfectly normal life.

From the children's ward I went on to night duty on the same observation ward where I had lain flat for two weeks of Christmas 1939. As we sat there in the semidarkness at the nurses' desk every sound brought back vivid memories and I wondered what change of circumstances would change my life. Would I ever return to study at my convent school desk, or had God in his wisdom arranged this mysterious illness? Even then, I had pictured myself as a successful nurse one day wearing the blue and silver badge that the lovely staff nurse wore who had attended to me so lovingly those dark long nights as I lay there. Even then I hated night duty, and longed for the day when I could come out of hospital altogether into the community for good. I knew that in order to qualify I should have to bear it for the next two years. I loved the mornings, though, especially having a nice breakfast and chat with my friends, and the thought of going to a nice warm bed. I hated nights when it was time to get up. Night duty then was twelve hours with just one night off in seven. We also were expected to attend lectures in the morning after night duty. To me, this seemed pointless, as more often than not we fell asleep at our desks.

In my third year, before I sat my state finals, I was in charge of an acute illness male surgical ward where I often had to shave a male patient's private parts in preparation for the operating theatre. There was no modern blood transfusion apparatus then, so all blood and saline was infused from glass bottles. I remember going round in fear and dread counting the drips, praying and hoping it would not block. As well as that we had to be ready to cope with three visits from the night superintendent. I always felt she looked down on us poor students and dared anyone to fall asleep on duty. However, she did give me a very good report at the end of my three months' stint on that ward.

My worst three months during my two years' general training were in the theatre, where if you were not quick enough the surgeons swore at you. One day I walked out in between operations and almost gave up my career. Thankfully, the matron later begged me not to leave and give up such a worthwhile profession. I went back and sat my finals. I'm glad I did!

In February 1946 I sat my state finals, and six weeks later I had the happy news that I had passed. Naturally, I was over the moon. This was something I had studied for and waited so long for, and great was my joy to be able to wear the coveted blue and silver badge on my chest. The next three months I spent on night duty staffing on the maternity ward, but like the theatre, I did not like it much and decided not to do midwifery training, but then what? At that time, so soon after the war finished, we were asked whether we did not wish to stay at our training school staffing. I found the maternity ward too taxing for me. One night, together with three of my close friends, I decided to go to London as a postgraduate and study for the qualification in fever nursing. At that time there were outbreaks of poliomyelitis, tubercular meningitis, diphtheria and smallpox. Each of us applied separately to an advertisement in the *Nursing Mirror* and filled in our application forms, and as we were doubly qualified, it would just last one year. Thankfully, following interviews we were all accepted, and during May 1946 we commenced our fever training at Hither Green Hospital, London.

Because we were doubly qualified, I was put in charge, on the children's ward, after two nights' initial training, where at that time many died from diphtheria and whooping cough. It certainly opened my eyes to the danger of these diseases, when most of my twelve hours on night duty was spent lifting one child after another who were literally choking and gasping for breath. Often during the night I had to assist a doctor who had to perform a tracheotomy for diphtheria and where I was responsible that the tube was kept clear from mucus, otherwise the child would suffocate.

The saddest night of all during fever training was when a seventeen-year-old girl died in the early morning when I was in charge. She was admitted unconscious at 1 p.m. Diagnosis? Poliomyelitis or meningitis. Her symptoms were such that it could have been either. It was that very hot summer of 1947, when everyone who could swim did so to cool themselves. The girl's parents said she had been swimming the previous week. The consultant in charge pumped all the well-known vaccines into the patient. Sadly, she died at four the next morning, while I, together with her parents, sat at her bedside. They were absolutely distraught. So was I, but I could not show my feelings. Furthermore, because she died while I, was in charge, I had, for the first time, to attend the postmortem. I shall never forget how cold I felt that morning as I watched them one after another remove every organ from this young girl's body to find out why she had died. However, the only abnormality found was an enlarged heart. Verdict: Died from a benign illness.

During that year, too, a young man age twenty-seven, was admitted with meningitis, which, sadly, turned out to be the tubercular type, for which in that year there was no known cure, and despite tender loving care and hope, this young man faded away to a skeleton and died twenty-one days later. This worried me greatly, and inwardly I thought, *What a waste of a young life.* During that postgraduate year many times I felt like giving up my Catholic faith. I was questioning God and angry with Him, who had allowed this to happen.

During a night duty stint I did charge work on a ward of thirty men, all in various stages of tuberculosis. I always had a dread of contracting this disease from childhood. I knew and remembered many young people who died in a sanatorium near my home in Ireland. Even in 1947, there were many who were receiving the limited drugs available and died from the disease. One such young man, age twenty-six, was dying when I came on duty. Having received the report, I went in to see him and check his pulse. I was unhappy with his condition and called the houseman to come and see him. He thought the same as I did and ordered an injection of morphia to ease the patient's distress. Having had the drug checked by the doctor, I injected the patient and made him as comfortable as possible. Less than thirty minutes later I went back, checked his pulse, and proceeded to turn his pillow when suddenly he grabbed me like a vice, with immense strength, and I could hardly tear myself away. I did manage it and gently laid him back on his pillow. Less than thirty minutes later, he too died while I held his emaciated hand. Again I was devastated!

Looking back on that year in fevers, I found it to be the most challenging and demanding of my whole life, because I was so close to children and young people dying of diphtheria, whooping cough, meningitis, poliomyelitis and tuberculosis. At night while I was in charge I felt as if I was living with death, and each morning when I came off duty I gave thanks to God for the many who recovered.

At the end of the year I sat the examination for the qualification in fevers. I sailed through the theory examination, but I was within a hair's breadth of failing the practical examination where I had to prepare trolleys for operations. For instance, I was asked to prepare a trolley for a mastoidectomy. For a minute I could not remember the instruments used. I hated practical examinations, but loved theory. Fortunately, I did well in the Viva, the individual oral exam connected with state or university exams. I passed; now I was the proud owner of three nursing certificates.

At that time I still did not want to do midwifery, and after a holiday in Ireland with my family I applied and was accepted to study for the Queens Institute of District Nursing Sisters. I came to study in Leicester City for that certificate, which only lasted six months, but you had to agree to practise for one year after qualifying. I loved every minute of that training. We lived in a large Georgian house on a tree-lined side street called New Walk. After London, it seemed to me like Heaven. There was a matron who looked strict and Victorian but was very kind. On our day off we could have our breakfast in bed, which I loved. You prepared your tray the night before, and your friend brought it up.

After hospital this home and work was like living in Heaven, and one night during my year there I had a most beautiful dream. I dreamt I was in Heaven, but I was still doing the nursing in the homes of the people whom I loved – that to me was Heaven. During that year, too, for the first time in my life I mastered the art of riding a push-bike, and needless to say, I spent hours on and off duty riding. I felt just as important as royalty pedalling round the picturesque Leicestershire countryside with the many delightful friends I made in Leicester. At the end of the six months' training I sat the examination for the Queens Institute and passed.

My year's contract in Leicester City flew by because I was so happy doing the job I loved in the homes of the people. At that time, late 1947, there was a fixed charge for the services of the Queens Sisters. On completion we were responsible for collecting the fee and giving a receipt, which we handed over to Matron when we gave our report. This task was no longer necessary when the National Health Act was passed in 1948.

Our duties varied between medical, surgical and geriatric cases referred to us by the doctor, the hospital and, rarely, a request from a patient's relatives. We left the home each morning at 8.30 a.m. with our list of cases for the day. The more urgent ones were done first, the others in turn. We returned for a cooked lunch, which was served promptly at 1.30 p.m. and always presided over by the matron, who sat at the head of the table and served the meat course, having first said grace before meals. At 2.15 p.m. we each in turn gave Matron our morning's report on our visits, stressing cases who needed an evening visit. After our reports we rested until 4.00 p.m., when afternoon tea was served. At 4.30 p.m. we left again to do the evening visits. Often we had one or two cases of carcinoma, which needed injections of morphia. These were left until 7 pm, in the hope that the patient and relatives could get a rest.

One afternoon each week was set aside when we cleaned and replenished our black bags with sterilised instruments. There were no prepared surgical packs then; all the dressing had to be autoclaved and the surgical instruments boiled.

At the end of the year's contract, some of the sisters stayed on in the job. If not, you were obliged to move on to do further training, for instance, midwifery or health visiting, but then in order to be accepted for that certificate you needed part one of the Central Midwives Board certificate.

CHAPTER TWO

I applied to Leeds Maternity Hospital to study for part one midwifery. This hospital was attached to Leeds Medical School, so had a high reputation as a teaching hospital. I filled in the application forms and sent them off. Following a favourable interview, I received a letter to say I was accepted. I hated the thought of leaving Leicester, the Queens Home, and all my friends, yet I knew if I wanted to climb the ladder midwifery would be essential.

Two days before I left for Leeds, Matron and my friends at the Queens Home held a farewell party for me in the lounge, where there was a lovely display of food and flowers. The music was played on a wind-up gramophone. There were some nostalgic records of the late John McCormack, whom I loved to listen to and often played secretly in our rooms at night when we were supposed to be in bed. Needless to say, I cried my eyes out and could not eat a thing. Towards the end of the evening I perked up, having been to my room and washed my face and powdered my nose. I had to look decent because the examiner from the institute headquarters in London came down for the night to present me with a ten-pound textbook on midwifery as well as a bouquet of carnations. Again I wept uncontrollably, and I was comforted by the matron and the lovely lady examiner. I shall always remember that evening with mixed feelings and wondering if I was doing the right thing.

Two days later I bade a fond farewell to all my friends on Leicester station and boarded the 3.50 train for another journey into the unknown. Thankfully, I slept most of the way, because for the last two nights I had not slept. Soon the guard shouted, 'The next stop is Leeds central station!' I jumped up, gathering all my belongings, ready for getting out. I felt dreadful inside but knew it was pointless, so made a dash to the taxi rank.

After I had waited about five minutes, a very jovial taxi man asked me where I wanted to go.

I replied, 'Leeds Maternity Hospital, Hyde Terrace,' to which he replied, 'Madam, is it safe to go by taxi, or should I call an ambulance?'

I had to smile, saying, 'I'm not in labour. I hope to train

as a student midwife.'

Less than ten minutes later we were outside a huge dark grey building that reminded me of the old workhouse I remembered when I was a child in Ireland. I was so nervous I was shaking as I rang the bell on the outer door of the nurses' home. Soon it was opened by a nurse who invited me to come in and sit down to await the home sister.

Less than five minutes later a very stately figure arrived wearing a grey uniform and a frilled hat. She introduced herself as Sister Kemp, saying, 'I'm the home sister, and I shall look after you during your six months here. Do not be afraid to discuss your worries with me – I can usually help.' She ushered me into a huge dining hall where I met three more homesick students who had arrived an hour earlier, and one of them was crying.

Following a cup of tea we were allocated our bedroom in the nurses' home. On first sight it looked small and bare. The bed was only two feet, six inches wide, and apart from a study desk, chair, and wardrobe there were few luxuries to wallow in. By suppertime I felt a lot better, especially as I had a lot more qualifications than the others had; many of them had come straight from the general hospital where they trained.

I slept fitfully and dreaded the morning when I had to report for duty to the acute ward where all the most difficult cases were admitted. However, it was much better than I imagined, and the sister seemed cheerful and kind. The procedure for a student midwife was that you had to watch ten normal deliveries before you were allowed, with strict supervision, to deliver your first baby. That same morning at 11, I watched my first baby being born. The experience was terrific, but the pain and anguish on the mother's face put me off ever marrying or having a baby myself.

By the end of two weeks I had witnessed ten normal deliveries, and later that day the sister told me to be prepared to deliver my first baby. In order to qualify for that, you had to take the complete history from the mother and gain her confidence in you. All the history in detail had to be recorded in your own personal delivery book; then you had to proceed to record the blood pressure, palpate the abdomen, and listen to the foetal heart, making sure of the position of the baby and whether the head was engaged in the pelvis ready for a normal delivery. The sister was quite pleased with my approach and verdict. During labour I was responsible for the complete care of the mother.

At five that evening the sister called me, saying the mother was fully dilated, and instructed me to scrub up and prepare to deliver the baby. I was terrified as I gowned and masked for the most important moment of my life, secretly muttering the *Hail Mary*. The mother did everything she was told at the right time, namely, pushing, relaxing, and panting. At 5.45 p.m. I delivered my first baby girl safely and without a tear. Inwardly, I was ecstatic, thanking God and feeling great. Afterwards I swabbed the mother and for the first time bathed a newborn baby. I felt ten feet tall!

During the next four months, I delivered my full quota of babies and recorded them in my personal delivery book. Only one out of the twenty needed help, and such babies were delivered safely with the help of forceps; this method of delivery was always carried out by a doctor of obstetrics.

I was glad when the six-month midwifery training was at an end, because Leeds was a black industrial city, especially the Hyde Terrace end. All my underclothes were sooty black after only one day, and the cost of soap powder was expensive on a student midwife's meagre salary. The one thing I liked most about Leeds Teaching Hospital was attending all our lectures at Leeds University with the medical students. At the end of the six months I sat the hospital midwifery examination, which I passed, and received my hospital midwifery certificate. I kept it safely with my valuables, and even today I often look at it with pride. A week or so later I sat the state midwifery examination at the hospital and the practical examination I did at the Jessop Hospital, Sheffield. For that I was handed a bucket containing a human placenta, which I had to examine and answer questions on the normal and abnormal blood vessels in the placenta itself. Even though I had doubts about my answers, they must have satisfied the examiners, because I passed both the theory and practical examination of part one.

3

I was the ninth child born into a family of eleven – six boys, five girls – in the 1920s to a wonderful mother and an alcoholic father, whom I only remember seeing once before he died when I was seven. He was in and out of hospital for years with rheumatic heart disease, and also very bad leg ulcers. The rheumatic heart condition was thought to result from alcohol abuse and lying drunk in wet ditches at night.

I remember vividly the day the green telegram came to Mother saying my father was seriously ill in the hospital twenty miles away. Though I was just seven, I was busy making hot drinks for my mother, who was recovering from pneumonia, lying in the settlebed in the kitchen. She read the telegram, and I recall the little boy who delivered it asking my mother was there a message to be sent back, to which my poor mother replied, 'I'll try and get to the hospital'. Less than two hours later, the same boy came with a second telegram saying my father had died.

My brother was sent to fetch my cousin, who was in his twenties, to discuss first, how my sick mother was going to reach the hospital, because there was no transport and there was only one person in the parish who had a motorcar at that time, but he was also the postmaster for our parish. My cousin went to ask this man, Alec Anderson, if there was any way he could help. Being a good Protestant man, he agreed to take my mother to the hospital so the removal of the body and funeral could be arranged. When my mother and Alec saw my father laid out in the mortuary in a cold shroud, my mother, having brought my father's favourite warm shirt, kindly asked the attendant if he would remove the shroud and put the shirt underneath? He refused, but Alec Anderson said curtly, 'You heard what the lady said,' and the attendant immediately helped my mother to put my father's shirt on.

The night of my father's death our house was full to overflowing with kind neighbours who came to sympathise with my mother, who, because of her illness and the trauma of her journey to the hospital to arrange my father's funeral was barely able to stand on her feet. Despite her weakness, she treated everyone who came to our poor house with either a drink, or tea and ham. Most of the Protestants and Catholics who came did not come empty-handed, each carrying a sack of flour, wheatmeal and lots of lovely potatoes and green vegetables. One neighbour who had recently killed a pig brought a half-side of bacon, enough to feed us all for several weeks. That night my sister and baby brother and I were allowed cocoa with a lovely slice of homemade bread for our supper. Normally, we would have oatmeal porridge and fresh buttermilk for our supper. I remember Teresa and Peter falling asleep on our neighbour's knee. We could not go to bed because our settlebed where we all slept was being used as a seat.

The following day was our father's funeral and burial, preceded by a requiem Mass at our local church. At 10 a.m., a man arrived in a glass hearse pulled by two horses with my father's coffin inside the hearse. My poor mother broke down, then I did, because that was the first time I had seen my mother cry. Soon, however, I was hugged by a nice lady who was saying, 'Do not cry, darling. I'll look after you while your mother goes to the funeral.' She did cuddle us all in turn, giving us drinks of fresh cows' milk and bread. As I looked out of our small window the lane was crowded with men, women and children who would follow the cortège to our chapel, which was at least two miles away. Both Teresa and Peter cried, asking when Mother was coming back. 'Soon,' the kind lady replied. 'Dry your eyes and don't worry your mother.'

My mother and the relatives and neighbours returned

from the funeral to a table laden with sandwiches and cakes for the reception. I'd never seen so much food before, and being only seven, I had not seen what they were carrying because it was all wrapped up in a greaseproof paper. I prayed and hoped that there would be some left for Teresa, Peter and me. Soon with the help of the lady my mother made large pots of tea from a huge iron kettle that was boiling on the hearth turf fire. Yes, we all had plenty of nice things when our friends and neighbours left. That afternoon, however, I remember my mother looking sad and serious while she was talking to my male first cousin, though I was not supposed to be listening. I heard her say that in order to pay for Dad's funeral the yearling calf would have to be sold at the next fair day. I cried bitterly, because I loved that friendly calf.

In the months following my father's death, my mother had a neighbour's girl in to look after us while my mother, a nurse and midwife, had to accept any job that was offered to her, because in that era there were no governmental allowances whatsoever for families, so it was a case of take any work or starve. Often, in between delivering newborn babies and laying out the dead, my mother was employed by neighbour farmers to cut seed potatoes for planting, as well as tying hay and oats in July and August for a shilling a day if she was lucky. More often than not she was paid in kind. I remember her sitting down exhausted at night, falling asleep while trying to sew a piece of cotton so I could be sent to the national school, where I should have been long before the age of seven. On one occasion, after a thorough investigation, my mother was allowed a few shillings a week – poor law relief, it was called. However, that too was stopped, because someone told the relieving officer she was working.

In May that year I was prepared to go to school for the first time. I shall always remember the first day at school. It was a grey pebbledash (a rough stone coating) building separated by a wall from the boys' school. We never either mixed with the boys or strayed from our play yard to the boys' school. I remember, too, trying to read the inscription on the front wall, which read: DRUMGOSSATT NATIONAL SCHOOL BUILT IN 1891. Our school was staffed by a principal and an assistant teacher who was simply dressed in a cotton dress with a buckle belt. Her name was Miss Connoly, and that was how we were taught to address her at all times. The principal teacher was a rather more elegant figure dressed in a nice smart blue suit. Incidentally, she was also the wife of the postmaster and had three children who were cared for during the day by a servant girl. At the top of the yard there was a small building containing dry closets, which smelled dreadfully, so bad I hated ever using them, and which I kept down to a minimum of once a day.

I wore a simple cotton dress made by my mother the night before by the light of an oil lamp that hung on the wall. The little dress cost 6d a yard. I wore a new pair of white canvas shoes and long white stockings kept up by elastic garters. I remember feeling very nervous when I saw my fellow pupils and Miss Connoly, our teacher, who called me up to her desk and asked me how old I was and whether I had read any infant books? I said I had and that I had brought it to school. She replied, 'Good girl, that's what I like to hear.' She told me to sit in the high infants' class. I had hardly got to my little chair when she approached me, taking my book and asking me to spell little words such as *cat, dog, house and cow*. I could read and spell all of the words in my book. The teacher smiled at me and promptly placed me in the first class, saying, 'There is no need for you to waste time in high infants; you seem to know more than most of them in the first class.'

In June the same year as I started school I joined the First Communion class, where we were prepared spiritually for the greatest day of our young lives, when we made our first confession and met Jesus for the first time in Holy Communion. I loved the intensive spiritual preparation. It was customary to be dressed in a special white dress, veil and white shoes and long white stockings. My poor mother did not know how she was going to be able to get either the material or shoes, which were expensive. However, two weeks before the great day, a friend of ours came home on holiday from England with all the lovely things that I could ever have wished for. The dress was made of ivory satin, with long sleeves and frills round the skirt. Needless to say, I was so excited I could not prevent myself when mother was out from going to see if my beautiful dress was still there. Sometimes I thought it was a dream!

At last the great day arrived. It was a beautiful morning and the first Saturday in June. Even though in those days you were obliged to fast from midnight the night before, I was not feeling hungry, but could not wait to put on my beautiful dress. I shall always remember with joy and gladness the smile on my mother's face, saying as she hugged me, 'Never forget to pray for the kind benefactor who made this day possible for you and me.' As we walked the two miles to the chapel, everyone we met along the way stopped and many of them put a new sixpence in my hand. This I handed over to my mother to be spent on groceries. At last we reached the chapel, where all the first Communicants were in the front seat before the high altar. Our teacher came to meet me, smiling and saying, 'You look like a fairy princess.' I felt every inch a princess, because no one else had such a dress in the class of thirty that day.

One by one we approached the altar to receive the body of Christ. Our teacher stood behind each one of us in case we dropped the host. I felt slightly nervous when the priest approached me.

As soon as we arrived home from the ceremony, I sadly had to remove both my beautiful dress and shoes before I had my lovely breakfast. Because of the special occasion I had a lovely fresh-boiled egg, tea and homemade bread and butter. I was so hungry from the long fast, I wanted to go on eating. Why this day and breakfast was so special was that apart from Easter Sunday, we rarely had an egg for breakfast. My mother had to sell them to buy the weekly groceries, as she did with the butter from our one cow. In the spring when the eggs were plentiful, the price was down to five pence a dozen. Some weeks she sold twelve dozen, which meant there was just twelve shillings to buy the goods for four of us. Thankfully, we always had fresh vegetables in our garden as well as milk in the summer when our cow calved.

I loved school subjects and had no difficulty in passing many of my friends who had been at school for two or more years before me. Towards the end of June each year we sat exams on all subjects before being promoted to the next class. I moved higher every year until I reached the sixth class, which was as far as we could go in the national school. When I was thirteen, I sat a scholarship for the private convent school where, if you passed, you were accepted as a boarder. At that time parents who could pay had their children educated at the high school, and the cost was only fifty pounds per year. In August that year I was told by our teacher that I had passed the test for the convent school, where I could start in September and continue studies for my intermediate and matriculation examinations.

That particular day I felt as if I were walking on air, rushing home to tell the great news to my mother, who, of course, was also delighted, but straight away her face changed as she said, 'But how or where will the money come from to buy your uniform and bed for the convent?'

Being so young, I said, 'Perhaps they will be buying blackberries this year.' I knew I must get there somehow, but I did not know how I could! Nothing short of a miracle could help me now; only God could, and he did.

That year, the jam factory in our town was buying blackberries and paying the princely sum of one shilling a stone for clean blackberries. By 'clean' they meant they did not want bits of the bush of the berry, because that would increase the weight. Fortunately, the month of August that year was lovely and dry, so from early morning Mother and I travelled our fields to pick all the blackberries as they became ripe. By lunchtime on good days we used to have two large tin buckets ready for sale, and as soon as we ate our few potatoes and milk we were off again to the fields to gather sometimes until dusk, when it was so dark you could not see the berries. On good days we managed to pull four stone, which would mean roughly four shillings a day. Both Mother, sister Teresa, and I were so exhausted by the end of the day we could barely carry our laden buckets home. After a cup of tea and an egg, which we had at the hearth fire, often we fell asleep there and could hardly get ourselves into the old settlebed with the chaff tick. I slept solidly until Mother nudged me at 8 am to get up for another laborious day in the fields. Thank God by the first week in September we had collected enough money for both my uniform and books, which we had to buy as well. It was a Thursday and our market day in our town when Mother and I proudly set off for the three-mile walk to where we were going to buy all my clothes for the start of term at the Convent of St Louis, Carrickmacross. As we walked along the country road I felt on top of the world when suddenly we saw an elderly man in a car slow down, asking if we would like a lift to the town, Mother said, 'Yes, we would be most grateful.' It was our friendly Protestant minister from our parish in Magheracloone, who knew my mother very well from her work as both a nurse and labourer helping out farmers in the parish. During the journey he asked which school I attended. Mother told him that I had won a scholarship for a free place at the convent. He turned round to me, saying how happy he was to hear the great news, and wished me every success in the future.

It was 9 September and the great day that I thought would never come had at last arrived. I remember it was a glorious morning and all my goods and belongings were packed ready to go. A kind neighbour with a horse and cart came to transport Mother and me as well as my bed and linen to Carrickmacross, where I was to stay and study hard until I was sixteen. I remember as the horse and cart left our old house on the bog road all the neighbours in the vicinity were out on the bank waving us off and some of them even shoved a silver sixpence into my hand, though many of them were as poor as we were. Soon we reached the main Carrick Road, where we passed many people we knew carrying their butter and eggs to the market there. It brought many memories of the times I helped my mother to carry ours to the same market.

The church clock in Carrick was striking 3 p.m. when the old horse with its load trudged up the church hill to the convent school, where we saw many of my fellow pupils getting out of posh pony traps and one or two cars. Even then I could not help thinking and wondering how I could compete with them, because most of their parents were paying the fifty pounds for their board and education and I had won a place there free. I even thought that the sisters might be more lenient and helpful educationally to the pupils whose parents were paying, yet I knew indirectly I was also being paid for.

Mother went up the steps and rang the big doorbell, and the door was soon opened by a young novice in a white veil who welcomed us into the parlour to await the Reverend Mother, who to me looked very imposing in her habit. The convent handyman helped our kind neighbour to unload the iron bedstead and mattress. The young novice showed them where in the long dormitory to put my little two-foot-wide iron bed. I was allowed back in the parlour with my mother and neighbour, who by then were having tea and cakes. I longed to join them, but the boarders' tea was laid in the refectory for 4 pm.

The young novice led me into the refectory, where the tables were laid for our tea. I nearly lost my life when I saw the line of bare tables with cups and saucers and side plates that each contained two slices of bread and one pat of butter and jam together with a small cake. I then burst out crying and wanted to run back to Mother, but the young novice came and put her arms around me, saying, 'Bridget, please dry your eyes. I felt just like you ten years ago when my mother left me here at this same school. Look at me now! I'm so happy in the religious life, and this school is home away from home.'

I sat beside a pleasant girl called Bernadette Trynor who was starting her second term. She comforted me by touching my hand under the table, saying, 'In a few days you'll love it here, and I'll always be your friend.' From that moment on I felt so much better and wanted to spend more time with Bernadette. Sadly, she was a term ahead of me, so I did not see her during the day except at mealtimes, which I always longed for so I could sit beside my friend.

CHAPTER THREE

After the first few days I settled down, but found the regime of the convent very hard and strict after the country school where I had spent my life for five years. There was really no comparison. For instance, after my first night from Monday to Saturday after tea we had to spend one and a half hours doing prep, with a sister always in the classroom watching our every move, and any talking or whispering to one another was soon quelled. Sunday, however, was a little easier. After Mass and lunch we went for a long walk in the country supervised by two sisters who walked behind us. When we returned, we had our tea, which on Sunday always consisted of a special treat of a homemade scone and jam. I liked that because it reminded me of Mother's delicious currant cake, which we always had on Sunday for tea. After our tea we wrote a letter to our parents telling them how we were getting on and all other interesting news.

Christmas was a truly wonderful time when I was young. The preparations for Christmas did not really get going until the morning of Christmas Eve, when Mother got out the clean milk crock to mix the huge pudding that consisted of six large eggs and three bottles of Guinness. We children were each allowed to stir in turn, and to this day I've never forgotten the rich aroma of the mixture. When the huge mixture was ready it was put into a specially prepared calico bag, tied up and placed in a sweet tin the shopkeeper used to store his boiled sweets in. Provided you were a good customer, you could have one free. This tin was very useful for carrying milk and water from the spring well. We children loved Christmas Eve, because no porridge could be boiled that day, as the Christmas pudding had to be kept on the boil for seven hours. Beside it on the hearth fire the big black iron kettle hummed away, always ready to top up the pudding water round the tin can. That was one of the days in the year when we did not have porridge for our supper. Instead we had cocoa and a large slice of currant cake, which we loved.

Early on Christmas morning we made the two-mile walk to the chapel for the first Mass of Christmas, when the bells rang out in joyful jubilation to celebrate the birth of the Christ child. After the Mass and Holy Communion were finished, we walked back home enjoying the lovely crisp, frosty air, and somehow we always heard the song of the little birds, as if they knew it was Christ's birthday and they too were celebrating. As soon as we got home from Mass, having taken off our best coats, we sat around a roaring turf-and-log fire on the hearth awaiting our special breakfast, which consisted of a thick slice of Christmas pudding fried in the same pan as the bacon. That, with a mug of sweet tea, was delicious and filling; small wonder I loved Christmas so much. Following breakfast we looked in our long black stockings to see what Santa had brought us. It usually was an apple, an orange and a few sweets, which we had to keep until after dinner.

During my first year at the convent, being a scholarship student, I had to put up with a lot of stick from the rich paying students, who never failed to remind the comparatively few free students that their parents could not pay the fees for their education. What they failed to understand, however, was that we won our place on the merits of our hard work and the state was paying our fees. There were many nights during my first year when I cried myself to sleep as soon as the sister left our dormitory. Bernadette was a staunch friend all through this very unhappy period, even though her parents were paying the fee for her. When we were alone together she often used to tell me, 'Never mind, Bridget. They are only jealous of your brains, wishing they could do the subjects like you.' I was so appreciative of her kindness and understanding that often, unknown to many of the others, I helped her with maths and spelling, which she was pretty weak on. Often the nuns used to keep her in after we had gone to do them over again.

At last, it was the last day of term and we were going home for the Christmas holidays. My mother had walked the three miles into town to fetch me. I dreaded the long walk home, wondering how I was going to carry all my bits and pieces together with my books, but the sheer excitement of seeing my mother and family, together with Christmas, kept me going. My mother was given my end-of-term report, and even though I had an idea I'd done reasonably well, I was still nervous. Soon, however, I had a message saying my mother was in the parlour waiting for me, also that a kind neighbour was waiting to take us home. I was even more overjoyed when Mother told me it was the same kind Church of Ireland vicar who gave us a lift before. I was so delighted to see my mother I fell into her arms, saying, 'What does my report say, Mother?' to which she replied, 'I'm very proud of you, Daughter. Keep it up, please, and you'll do well.'

The next day, the Feast of Saint Stephen, was also a wonderful day for us, because it was known as the Wren day, when all the young men around the country dressed up in fancy costumes and called at all the houses, where they were invited in to have a slice of Christmas pudding and a bottle of stout. Having refreshed themselves, they sang and danced Irish jigs on our clay floor. At first, we were afraid of them, but Mother told us they were only Wren men acting out the custom on Saint Stephen's Day. (What innocent fun it all was then compared to today. All our doors were left on the latch for any neighbour to call in for a chat and a mug of tea).

Soon the holidays were over and it was time for me to return to the convent boarding school for another year's hard work. Mother took me back on 7 January, and I remember vividly I broke down and cried as we walked up the convent path, but Mother cuddled me saying, 'Never mind, dear, it will soon be Easter, when you can come with me to the fields and help the farmers.' As soon as the door opened and I saw my favourite sister I stopped crying and fell into her arms, saying, 'Sister, I love you. Will you always be my friend?' to which she replied, 'Of course, I will, my dear. Now pull yourself together.'

I turned round and saw my friend Bernadette coming to greet me, saying, 'Did you have a good holiday and what did Santa bring you?' I replied, 'I had fruit and sweets. What did you have?'

Dette said, 'I had a Christmas baby doll, which opens and closes her eyes.'

I replied, 'How lovely, Dette. I hope one day I'll be able to see her.' That's always something I should have loved to have, but knowing how my mother had to struggle to keep us

I never expected to have one. However, that same year friends of ours home on holidays from England brought me a doll. It was small and pink, without hair, but as soon as I held it up its eyes opened and they were sky blue. I was so happy I cried with joy. I looked after her so tenderly and lovingly like a real baby. During our sewing lesson I made her a pretty dress and pants to match, also a sweet little bonnet to cover her bare head.

The spring term just flew, and it was time to go home again. I did not look forward to it one bit – in fact, I really dreaded it – knowing I should have to help my mother with our neighbouring farmers setting their potato crops. I could not comprehend how I should know what to do. The job I dreaded most was cutting seed potatoes for planting, though Mother was a dab hand at that job and was wanted by every small farmer in the neighbourhood for twelve hours cutting seed potatoes. Even though I was not yet thirteen, I used to think how sad it was that my mother should have to do that type of menial work for about a shilling a day, but with dire poverty about very few could afford a midwife to deliver their babies. Instead, they had the nearest handy woman who happened to be there at the time of the birth. This state of affairs often had tragic results, mainly because of the lack of hygiene both before and during the delivery. My mother, when she was engaged for a delivery, rarely got paid in cash; often it was a bag of potatoes or flour. That was for fourteen days' hard work looking after the mother and baby.

At last, Easter day arrived, and it was a really glorious day. Mother had made a lovely Christmas pudding; also that day we could have as many fresh eggs as we could eat. If the weather was good Mother made a big fire in our field, where the tea was made and the eggs were boiled in a huge saucepan. Then, following grace before the meal, we sat around an open fire thoroughly enjoying the feast of fresh boiled eggs with lots of good homemade bread, butter and damson jam. We never had chocolate eggs as children; instead, friends and neighbours gave us fresh eggs as Easter presents. Often they felt warm in our little hands as we rushed joyfully home to give them to Mother to keep for us until Easter day. Even now I often reflect how happy and innocent we were then. Violence, mugging and burglaries were unheard of; you could go out for the day and leave your door on the latch.

The next week potato planting was in full swing again with all the small farmers in our neighbourhood wanting my mother to cut their seed potatoes. She was so good at cutting seed the news got round; although they seemed to forget she had only one pair of hands. I soon learned the hard way. At first, I had to let my mother see how I had done it before the crop was put in the planting bag that went out to the field for the potato droppers. She taught me the importance of making sure there were three or more eyes on the seed in order to get a good crop of potatoes for the whole year. I was very slow to begin with, but the second week I gathered pace and I became quite quick, and my mother was very pleased with my progress. There was one great advantage about working for farmers – you had your dinner and tea, which was just as well, because by the time we got home at dusk we were both exhausted and could only just manage a quick cup of cocoa and to throw ourselves into the old settlebed in the kitchen.

The second week of my vacation, weather permitting, Mother and I spent the long days dropping seed potatoes in the open drills in front of the planter. By evening, both our backs were so painful that we had to take an Aspro with our cup of cocoa, after which we both fell asleep on the stool in front of the old turf fire. We were so exhausted when we fell into bed, we did not even notice the lumps in the old chaff tick. To this day in my late sixties I suffer from lower back pain. Small wonder; considering I was only thirteen, my bones and joints were soft and easily injured. Needless to say, the last day of dropping the potatoes I thanked God I was going back to my convent school.

The farmer for whom we worked took me back to school accompanied by my mother. I nearly ran to the front door with my little case, so glad to be back again to study instead of doing labour, but it had helped my mother, as well as getting me some new things I wanted. As I said goodbye to my mother, she pushed a ten-shilling note into my hand and I felt like a millionaire.

About three days into the term the headmistress sent for seven pupils in my class, including me, to come to her study. We were very worried, thinking we had done something wrong. Instead, it was to say she was putting us forward for a Gaelic scholarship, which if we won would mean a whole month in Ranafast, a Gaelic-speaking college in Donegal, as well as the Gold Fainne, which we could always wear with pride on our dresses. We were all delighted to be picked to study for this honour. Mother did, however, instil into us the task we were about to undertake, because so many thousands sat each year for that coveted Gold Fainne. Sister told us the scholarship class would commence next week. Then I wrote to my mother to tell her the great news. She replied straight away, congratulating me and saying how hard I should have to work to get it, because all the study for the oral and Viva would be in Gaelic and the standard required was very high. I was so happy I could not wait to get started!

The following week our Gaelic teacher took us for one hour in the morning and likewise in the afternoon. Then during our prep in the evening we had to put the language into practice. Though it was hard, I loved it and the challenge of the end result; also the thought of getting away for a whole month in August was exciting. I worked every spare moment on my Gaelic, practising on my class friends, speaking in the Gaelic language much of the time. For the six weeks preceding the exam we had stiff oral and Viva tests in our hour with the sister who was preparing us for the scholarship. I found it very hard, but the challenge was too exciting to miss and I worked like mad every hour of every day until the great day arrived.

To sit the exam itself we had to travel to a convent school in Monaghan, which was twenty miles away. On the ordinary service bus we were chaperoned by two sisters from our school. On arrival at Monaghan Convent we were ushered into a sparse classroom, and only then the nerves in my stomach played me up and I felt I could not answer the questions on the paper. Thankfully, however, all my studying

CHAPTER THREE

paid off and I found no difficulty in completing the exam.

On the way home, all my school chums and I were agog and could speak of nothing else, except discussing the questions and how we answered them. The din of our collective voices became so loud that the senior nun remonstrated with us, saying, 'Please be quiet, we are trying to read our office,' to which we all shouted together, 'Sorry, Sisters. We'll say no more,' but the silence was like penance to us.

Back at the convent following lunch, we each in turn discussed our questions and answers with our Gaelic-speaking tutor who had prepared us for this coveted scholarship for the past three months, as well as the honour of wearing the Gold Fainne, which every Gaelic scholar wore with pride. I described in detail what my answer was to each question, to which my tutor replied, 'If what you tell me is correct you stand as good a chance as the other three hundred students. However, never become too complacent.' As I left her office I had an uncanny feeling inside me that I'd won.

On 23 June, three weeks later, the large buff envelope popped through the convent letterbox. My heart was in my mouth when at commencement of our Gaelic class our sister tutor proudly read out the names of the successful candidates in turn, giving us our percentage marks. When she called me forward and told me I topped the list with 85 per cent, I nearly fell face downwards on the floor with excitement and uttered, 'Thank God, I love you.' Sadly, two of our group failed to get the required mark. Suddenly all my joy faded into tears when I realised my best friend would not be coming with me. Bernadette was inconsolable and ended up in the sickroom for the rest of the day.

The next day was the end of term, and we all packed ready to go home the next day. As soon as I saw my mother in the drive I ran down and fell into her arms, saying, 'I'm going to Ranafast in August for a whole month.'

Though my poor mother was overjoyed for me at the back of her mind, the great worry was: 'How are we going to buy extra clothes as well as the train fare to Donegal?'

I replied, 'Mother, I'll work on the farm with you right up until I go.'

As soon as I settled at home, haymaking began with a vengeance, with all the local farmers wanting my mother's hay-tying skills, but they were not so sure that I could do the job. My mother sternly said unless I could come she would go elsewhere, so sooner than lose an expert they agreed I could come as well. The next day was dry and sunny, so Mother and I left home about 7.30 a.m. to start a day's hard labour for the princely sum of one shilling and sixpence for me. The total at the end of the week was a measly nine shillings, but even that was a lot, considering we were partially fed as well. After a few days I picked up speed and could keep up with the best of them. At the end of two weeks my mother made it plain to the farmer that my wages should be increased to one shilling a day for ten hours' labour. There was something lovely and homely about haymaking. I especially loved having our tea out in fields; it always reminded me of our picnics on Easter Sundays. From the middle of June right up to when I went to my college in Donegal, I worked solidly six days a week, and at the end of that time had saved enough money for some new clothes and my rail fare to Ranafast, the Gaelic-speaking college, where all my food and tuition would be taken care of.

The fifteenth of August arrived and a kind neighbour took me and my few belongings into Carrick to catch the morning train to Donegal, where I had arranged to meet my fellow students at the station. To this day, looking back, that was one of the happiest days of my life, the thought of coming back with the coveted Gold Fainne so wherever you went they knew you were a classic Gaelic scholar, an honour which no one could ever take away from you. Alas, that privilege was not to be mine because, being so poor, my mother could not find the five pounds to pay for it and it was not included in the scholarship. All the way home I cried bitterly, knowing that this coveted prize was still only for the well-off and I could never wear it on my lapel, as we were only allowed one week to get the money. So what was a great joy to me turned extremely sour, and to this day I have never come to terms that something that was won with sheer hard work should be lost because I happened to be born poor.

It was now 1938. I was sixteen, and in July that year I had to sit my intermediate exams. So from the middle of January I worked all hours studying the subjects and particularly the one I was weak on, i.e., maths. I loved English, Gaelic, history and science. Both my teacher and I knew that unless I concentrated on my maths, I might not even get a pass. As my whole life was geared to teaching as a profession, I knew I should have to get a reasonably good grade.

Late that year, however, a sister of Nevers came to our convent school and gave us the history of Saint Bernadette of Lourdes, the order wherein she was a sister and secondary school teacher. Her school was in Tonbridge, Kent, and was a private day and boarding school. During the talk she intimated that she was interested in students who might think they had a vocation to the religious life, preferably teachers and nurses. Before she left she gave us all a picture of Saint Bernadette with a prayer for vocations on the back.

That talk in 1938 when I was sixteen completely changed my life, so much so that I began to think that God might be calling me to join that order. I began to pray more fervently at Mass and prayers; sometimes I quizzed God to tell me what to do. During the Easter vacation, I discussed my feelings and thoughts with my mother, who at first treated them lightly and thought it was a childhood fantasy and would pass. However, towards the end of the vacation she could see I was changed. The Nevers sister promised to come back and see us in the autumn. I was so sure, I could not wait to see her again. True to her word, the French sister returned and asked us had we thought about what we discussed on her last visit. Our class teacher said we had discussed it in class, also with our parents. She told Sister there were two of us who were very interested in talking about it more fully with her. After lunch that day, Marie Farrelly and I were asked to go into the parlour and spend as much time as we wished finding all about the order and the religious life. When we came out I was ecstatic with excitement and I was more sure than ever that I wanted to enter that order.

The French sister stayed overnight at the convent, and the following day we were allowed to accompany her to see our parents and see what they thought. For Marie and me it was the most wonderful day of our life, going round in a car with a lovely sister. When we got to our house, Mother had a marvellous tea laid in the parlour and welcomed Sister with open arms. She loved talking to my mother, especially about her midwifery work. After tea we discussed in some detail what all this would mean, especially leaving home and going to a strange country, and on reflection I knew it would be little different from the teaching at the school we were attending. But it would mean studying French at their convent school in Tonbridge. I had already got three honours in my intermediate examinations, and Sister said that was more than enough qualifications for either teaching or nursing. However, we had another year in our convent to study and think about it. Meantime, she promised to be in constant touch with us and our parents.

All that year, 1938, as each day went by I could think of nothing else but the excitement of preparing to leave home for a new country. Often, however, it was also tinged with sadness at the thought of leaving Mother and my family. I could hardly comprehend what it would mean, but I had great faith that God would make everything possible. During the Easter holidays I developed a very sore septic finger, which was so painful I could not sleep. I became both low and depressed. Mother kept putting bread poultices on it, but it would not burst on its own. In the end our local schoolmaster took me in to the doctor, who lanced it straight away. Immediately the terrible pain was gone, and I felt great straight away. Soon we were home and outside our gate where this master suddenly touched my upper leg. Although I was innocent, I knew it was wrong, but I did not know at the time how you could become pregnant. Strangely enough, that month I did not menstruate on the day I should have and I really thought it was because he touched my leg. For the next few days I went through hell worrying, yet I could not tell my mother what happened. I remember going round our fields and kneeling down, begging God to let my period start. It did, of course, come on, but it was a few days late.

During that spring and summer, sometimes I did not know how I could come to terms with leaving my mother and family, as well as having the terrible worry of how or where the money would come from to get the clothes I needed for my new life in England, let alone the fare by train and boat. Both my mother and I wondered if the meagre wages we got from our neighbouring farmers for hard labour would suffice. I had to have all new clothes to travel with; even a cardboard case would cost about two shillings, and for that we would have to work whole days in the cold and heat of both spring and summer. For a time during that spring I became so low I almost lost my deep faith. In fact, at times I could not believe it would ever happen. There was the awful fear, too, that a war was ready to break out between England and Germany. My mother realised how I felt and, fearing I would have a complete breakdown, tried to cheer me up, saying, 'Cheer up, my child, and place all our worries in God's hands; only he knows best.'

By the end of May that year we heard from England that we had to be prepared to travel in early September, because a French teacher would be returning from Ireland from the summer vacation and she would be in charge of us. One day during the term the Reverend Mother sent for Marie and me to tell us the latest news about September. I became very anxious and I asked Reverend Mother if we would still be going even if war broke out. She replied, 'Not to worry, my child. Have faith in God and always remember what happens is best.' From that time onwards, and because I believed so much in this saintly woman, I felt better and I no longer worried but put my faith in God.

June twenty-ninth was the Feast of Saints Peter and Paul and the end of term and for Marie and me it was our last day at our convent school, so in the midst of feasting I felt very sad and weepy at saying goodbye to all our lovely teachers and the friends we had made in the last five years. At 3 pm, my mother arrived to take me home. She went to see the Reverend Mother, who told her that everything was finalised, including visas for our journey to England and the start of my voyage into the unknown. I remember when I bade farewell to the Reverend Mother, she put her arms around me, saying, 'Don't worry, my child. You will always do well whatever you decide to do; you did splendidly here.'

On our way home that day in the old cart, Mother said that hopefully, provided we got enough work, she would be able to buy my clothes for England at the beginning of August, but said in order to cut down on costs we would have to make most of them. I remember her saying jokingly, 'Don't grow too much, because I cannot afford a coat; that nappa blue coat and hat will do for travelling.'

I said, 'Mother, you need not worry. I'll work hard no matter what I'm asked to do, even though I hate farming work, especially tying hay and corn.'

The very next day both Mother and I were engaged by the local farmer for haymaking for the next two weeks. The only thing I liked about haymaking was having our tea beside a hay stack, which, as I said, reminded me of our Easter Sunday picnic, having our tea and boiled eggs outside. There was one vital thing missing, however – the lovely blazing fire, which Mother was a dab hand at lighting and keeping alive. By the fifteenth of August, during corn time, Mother said she thought we had saved enough money to go shopping the next week. Suddenly I had the butterflies fluttering inside my tummy, at the thought of my journey into the unknown and saying goodbye to my dear mother, sister and brother. I had grave doubts at times, wondering if I was doing the right thing; then I'd cheer up with the thought: *If Marie can do it, so can I.*

On the sixteenth of August, Mother and I set out to walk the three long miles to Carrick, our nearest market town, where we hoped to buy everything for the journey to England. We had not gone very far when a car pulled up and the driver asked us if we were going to the town. It was our friendly Church of Ireland minister, who often gave us a lift, for which we were eternally grateful, especially when we had a heavy bag. He inquired how I was getting on at the convent. I replied, telling him hopefully of what my plans were.

He said, 'How interesting. I hope that war between

England and Germany can be averted before you leave.'

I replied, 'I hope so, too,' thanking him for his concern always.

Though we bought material for everything we could make ourselves, such as dresses, nightdresses, and slips, Mother only had a ten-shilling note and a few coppers left for all the groceries we needed for the week. The money from our hard work for two months on a farm had gone for my clothes for England. Still, the farmer offered us a further week's work, as the blackberries would be ready for picking, provided shops were buying them for the jam factories. Thankfully, they were needing blackberries that year, and Mother and I worked like mad collecting them from morning till night so as to pay my passage to England and leave Mother with sufficient money to carry on when I was gone. It was a good season, and we were able to put a little nest egg aside for a rainy day. Sadly, there was still a good crop left when I had to leave. Mother said tearfully, 'Never mind, Daughter. I shall try and pick them myself to buy winter fuel.'

4

It was time to sit the part two midwifery examination of the Central Midwives, which I passed in 1950. At a farewell party before I left we student midwives performed a concert for the matron and staff. I sang and danced to 'MacNamara's Band.' It was a marvellous night and I hated leaving that happy period of my life behind. I cried my eyes out when I bade goodbye to the matron, her deputy and the midwifery sisters who had helped us to reach this goal painlessly.

The following month, after passing my final midwifery examination, I was appointed as a district midwifery sister to a town called Corby in Northamptonshire. This to me was a real challenge, and the thought of being alone in charge of two lives was daunting to say the least. I joined three other midwives and a general Queens sister in two council houses joined into one. We had a nice lady housekeeper who spoiled us and waited on us hand and foot. Whatever time of the day and night we came in, there was always something good in the oven. At that time in 1950, Corby was a booming industrial town with the famous Stewart and Lloyds steelworks. Mostly it was young families of Scottish origin who came down to Corby for the works. This meant that rarely a night went by without an anxious young father on the doorstep. At that time I was not a car driver, so I would hand him the gas and air machine and, I with my black bag, followed later on my push-bike. As a sister, unlike in hospitals, we had to carry on with our nursing cases the next day even though we might have been up all night. In the 1950s it was the rule that mothers were swabbed and douched twice a day for the first three days after delivery. We only had one day and night off in seven. What a change from today, when the mothers are in and out of hospitals like machines and rarely ever swabbed. I cannot help wondering if this inadequate postnatal care could in some way be responsible for so many cervical diseases today.

Six months later, rather tired of so much night and day work, I applied for work in the nearby town of Wellingborough, Northants, as a midwifery sister. I was successful and moved into a lovely large house with plenty of ground space. It was called Elsden Lodge and was right away from the district. Here too we were looked after by a lady housekeeper, called Mrs Rene, plus an assistant who looked after us when the chief housekeeper was off.

It was during my time in Wellingborough that I decided to take a course of professional driving lessons. The school was called Blanche Flowers School of Motoring, my driving instructor was called Mr Brown, and the course of eight one-hour lessons cost eight pounds. The same course today costs ninety-six pounds. Some days I did everything right and Mr Brown was delighted with my progress. Other days I could not do anything right. One such day my Mr Brown became so angry with me, shouting, 'Drive into the ditch if you must!' I was very shocked at his remarks, and the butterflies in my stomach were pounding away. Nevertheless, with my true professionalism, I said, 'If I do as you say, both of us will be badly hurt.' At the end of the course I felt in no way could I take the driving test, so I enrolled for a second lot of eight lessons. Without practice, lessons are not much good. I gradually improved during the second course, and Mr Brown applied for me to take the driving test.

At last the day of my driving test arrived. It was a Friday morning, and it was in the town of Kettering, Northants. I did not know Kettering very well; also, it was market day and the stall holders had their wares all over the streets. I was petrified and before long I made my first mistake by approaching a pedestrian crossing too fast; also my emergency stop was too jerky. I failed on those two points. While I was waiting to resit, I paid a qualified driver to give me some practice in the nurses' old car, which we had to share and we lovingly called Judy. This made all the difference, and by the time I resat I was quite confident that I would pass. That was until the same examiner that failed me in Kettering a month earlier sat beside me in the passenger seat. I nearly died of shock. However, he consoled me and said, 'Please start your car using all gears and drive away.' He was right – I was quite confident, and I did just that. When we stopped, he fired question after question after question on the Highway Code at me. I knew all the answers.

When he handed me the form, saying, 'Congratulations. You passed,' I felt like hugging him. Instead I drove Judy back to the test centre, where my superintendent was waiting to drive me back to Northampton in case I had not passed. She asked me did I wish to drive us back to Wellingborough?

I replied, 'No, I never wish to drive that car again.'

She replied, 'Oh, but you must.'

It was several weeks before I attempted to drive Judy to a maternity case. One day I plucked up enough courage, and I am glad I did!

I shall always remember that particular case. She was a young Catholic mother expecting her second child, at twenty weeks' gestation, and she had a show of blood but at that stage had no pains. I made her comfortable and sent for medical aid. Meantime, she started getting labour pains. Shortly after that she said, 'Sister, I feel as if I want to push.' I suggested she try to wait for the doctor's arrival, but the interval between the pains became more frequent and I knew there was nothing I could do. I scrubbed up and prepared to deliver the foetus and waited for the next pain, when she pushed out the baby. It looked like a skinned rabbit and tried to cry.

Through the transparent skin the little heart was pumping, and the mother said, 'Sister, is that my baby crying?'

I replied, 'Yes, it is.'

I cut the umbilical cord and wrapped the baby in a warm towelling nappy and laid it down by the fire. It weighed one pound, thirteen ounces. It that was today it could have been saved. I attended to the mother and made her comfortable while I awaited the doctor. That tiny scrap of humanity lived for half an hour.

Being a Roman Catholic, I gave the baby a conditional baptism with ordinary water, saying, 'I baptise you in the name of the Father, the Son, and the Holy Ghost.'

The doctor walked in casually saying, 'How are things, Sister?' in a posh accent, to which I replied, 'The baby lived for thirty minutes. It is down by the fire.' He, smirking, said, 'You know it could not possibly live,' to which I replied, in an equally posh accent, 'I too know that baby could not live, but while it did I could not possibly do anything to shorten its life.'

With that he left. I comforted the mother and carried the baby down to the father still wrapped in the warm nappy. That incident left a deep impression on my life as a midwife.

5

In 1951, I applied to Leicester City for a bursary to train for health visiting. I had all the qualifications, at that time the minimum being state registration and at least part one of the Central Midwives Board certificate. I had qualifications in fevers and tropical medicine as well as being a state-certified midwife. I had met many health visitors during the course of my work in Northamptonshire, because the health visitor took over the care of the mother and baby from us at fourteen days. Today the health visitor takes over at the eleventh day.

In due course I received the application forms, which I duly filled in together with the names of two referees, one of whom had to be our superintendent, to whom I was responsible here. One month later I was asked to attend an interview. As I sat outside waiting to go in, my heart was in my mouth, wondering what they were going to ask me. I was even more petrified when I entered the huge room and saw the big round table where several people sat who immediately started questioning me about my life, education, work and hobbies. I could be forgiven for thinking it was a job in the Foreign Office I was after. Following thirty minutes' gruelling I was asked to wait outside. While I waited I met Doris, another candidate. She too was petrified and looked rather old to be applying to study for such an important certificate. Suddenly the door opened and I was recalled and told by the medical officer of health that I had been accepted for the next school, which would commence in September, subject to a medical examination. I was ecstatic and could have leaped for joy. I went back to Wellingborough as if I were on air, and all the girls back at the Lodge were delighted, saying we must have a farewell party before I left. Even at that early stage there were tears welling up in my eyes at the thought of leaving this comfortable and happy accommodation. As a health visitor student I would have to find my own place to live, and with a small bursary I realised it would be tough for the next year. Still, having been born into poverty myself was something that would help me to face the new challenge ahead.

The last two months in Wellingborough flew by, and soon it was time to leave my comfortable nest. My friends here, true to form, arranged a large farewell party to which all the nurses and midwives in the area as well as our superiors were invited. Even as I dressed for the occasion, I was brokenhearted, and I could hardly control the tears as I entered the big room where the housekeeper had laid a beautiful spread. Inwardly, I thought to myself, *it will choke me*, and I worried, too, how I should give a vote of thanks to everyone. However, after a few drinks I plucked up courage and gave a sincere speech, at the end of which I did break down completely, having received my gifts, which, thankfully, were mainly book tokens. I already had a list of the books a student had to read during the course, one of which had to be a book by Anthony Trollope.

At that time it did not matter how many qualifications you had – you went back to student status and received the minimum to live on. On arrival in Leicester City I was directed to a convent, where I spent the first month together with speech therapy students and a few health visitor girls who came from different parts of England. During my first week there I often thought I wanted my head examined for undertaking such a gamble; at other times I cheered myself up by thinking, *Well, life is a gamble and if I do not try nothing will be gained.* A month later I moved from the convent to a small bed-sit room in a private bungalow three miles away from the city centre and from which I biked three times a day, for which I paid two pounds, nineteen shillings a week for my board and lodging. I remember the bed was two foot by six and for company I had a tiny radio. I felt very alone at times and did not find the studies easy either, because unlike nursing, it was mostly legal work, relating to the 1948 Children's Act. At that time this responsibility was covered by the health authority relating to fostering and adoption.

The course lasted three terms, and every week we were subjected to tests. I hated these tests, and sometimes I did badly and was told in no uncertain terms that if my writing and studies did not improve I would never pass the stiff examination of the Royal Sanitary Institute. From then on I used a Parker fountain pen for the tests, and this made a world of difference.

During the last three months I studied with friends, and I found that far more beneficial because we used to question one another. In that way I could retain the knowledge. During the last term we had constant tutorials, and I loved them, feeling I was coming to terms with what preventative medicine was all about, as well as the importance of good maternity and child welfare. The newly qualified health visitor was responsible for the health of the whole family, including schools in her area. Public speaking came into the course a lot, and during the final month each student had to study a subject and stand up in front of the tutor and class. I found this terrifying and when it came to my turn my mouth felt as if it had dried up and I could not even state the title of my talk. I felt happier when the tutor encouraged me to continue, saying, 'Don't worry; this happens to all of us at first.'

In the middle of April 1952, D-day arrived when we were to sit our exams for three days at the Royal Sanitary Institute in London, which lasted three days and two nights. Most of the theory was concerned with legal matters relating to the Children's Act. The third and final day were the oral and Viva examinations, which I felt very nervous about but I need not have done, because I seemed to have answered all the relevant questions satisfactorily. That same lovely spring afternoon, as I left the Royal Sanitary Institute, I felt as light as a feather blowing in the wind, having felt I had given of my best – the rest lay in the hands of God. I had arranged with a fellow student who was staying in London to let me know the results. Unlike all other state examinations, we only had to wait two days. I went off to spend a week with my mother in Ireland. Two days later the telegram arrived, which just said: 'Success.' I was overjoyed and fell into my dear mother's arms. My mother had the news published in our weekly paper, the *Dundalk Democrat*.

In May 1952, I took up my appointment with Leicester City as a health visitor and school nurse. During the first week I first visited a very deprived area of Leicester where it was known that the parents, through poverty and lack of education, frequently gave overdoses of antibiotics to their sick babies, sometimes ending in tragedy. During my first six months in the job I spent more time in the nearby police station and courts than in the houses. I soon discovered that the mothers who need us most never take advantage of our weekly child health clinics and a medical officer.

By the end of my third month in the job, one of my mothers had a baby who was premature, weighing only four pounds. This woman stayed in hospital for a month and when she was discharged she needed a lot of help. In fact, I visited every day the first week so by the Friday she seemed to be managing quite well.

The following week I went to visit her on the Tuesday, and rang the bell. This time, however, she seemed to take a long time to open the door. When she did, her words were: 'I am glad you came. I was just about to put my head in the gas oven; instead, I will make a cup of tea.'

I was shocked, saying, 'You do not mean what you say,' to which she replied, 'Yes, I mean every word of it.'

I believe that God sent me there that day. During our tea and chat she opened up, telling me about how unhappy she was in her marriage, saying every night her husband was in the pub drinking.

There was a very happy ending to that sad story. The little baby thrived and grew up to be a lovely young girl. I was honoured to be invited to her First Holy Communion and confirmation day. She was eleven the day of her confirmation, and I will never forget her asking me that day could she be my bridesmaid when I got married? I said, 'Yes, but, Moira, I may never marry. I am essentially a career person.' That I am glad to say, was reversed when in 1958 I walked down the aisle of the Church of the Most Blessed Sacrament in Leicester and Moira, together with three other bridesmaids, proudly walked behind me that happy day, thus fulfilling her dearest wish, to be my bridesmaid.

On another occasion, a vegetarian mother came to my clinic with her baby, who was being breast-fed and slept most of the day and night. Because the baby was not crying, the mother naturally thought that she was contented. However, I was shocked when the mother put the baby on the scales. At seven weeks she weighed only seven pounds, less than her birth weight. I remained calm, asking the mother to wrap the baby up and see our medical officer. Meantime, I told the doctor in advance what to expect. I rang the mother's doctor, who arranged to have a letter by 4.30 p.m. for the mother to take to the hospital. By 5 o'clock the same day the emaciated baby was admitted to the baby care unit just in time – one more day would have been too late. I thanked God that the baby was saved because her mother brought her to my clinic.

Those two cases alone made my twenty-five years in health visiting worthwhile. However, there were numerous occasions when I questioned deeply why I left my fulfilling midwifery post for this lonely, demanding job.

6

In October 1957, I was introduced to my future husband outside the sacristy door of Holy Cross Church as I went into a meeting of the Legion of Mary. I was, at that time, a vice president. Patrick Joseph Dunne was his name, and he originally hailed from Ennis in County Clare. From now on I shall refer to him as Pappy. That's what he liked to be called, because his dear late mother never called him by his full name. When the meeting finished, he walked me down to the town, where I left him to get his bus. I was ecstatic with happiness that night. I felt at long last I had met a man I could easily fall in love with. As we said goodnight, he had arranged to meet me the following Tuesday in town. I was on my cycle that night, but I had a new car, a little Ford Popular, which I had bought new for the princely sum of £499. He took me to his semi-detached house, which he had bought for his mother because she was getting old and lived in a small cottage in Ennis since the death of her husband twenty-three years before. Sadly, however, she only lived six months with Pappy; she could never get used to England and pined to return to her native Ireland.

I shall always remember that happy evening when Pappy took me to his home. I was a bit nervous at first, but he thought that one through and when we arrived his former landlady, Mrs Yates, was there to meet us. That was the calibre of the man I later married. He made tea for the three of us, and I shall always remember some of the cups were chipped, but I cannot remember what we had to eat; I was on cloud nine. Every now and then I had the feeling Mrs Yates was sizing me up. Even though she was old enough to be his mother, she had designs on Pappy.

After tea we sat round a roaring coal fire while he played all our favourite seventy-eight records, which included the late John McCormack, Richard Tauber and street singer Arthur Tracy. That happy night flew by, and soon it was 10 pm, and time for me to go home. I gave a lift home to Mrs Yates, affectionately known as Auntie Emma.

Three weeks later as we were about to say goodnight, Pappy proposed to me in a very beautiful way, asking me, 'Could you entrust your life in me?' and saying, 'You need not answer now, think about it.' I thought deeply about his proposal for one week. I felt deeply it was true love and my answer must be yes. We both came from the same background, where from a very early age high ethics and morals were of the utmost importance. He had been educated by the Christian Brothers at a private Catholic school in Ennis, and I was educated to a high standard by the Louis nuns. Pappy hoped to enter a seminary and study for the priesthood, but at the age of seventeen he developed pneumonia, which left him with asthmatic symptoms. Sadly, he had to forget the seminary.

I also had ideas of entering the religious life, and the open door was winning a scholarship that enabled me to have a first-class education for free. I still hoped when I came to the convent in Kent in 1939 that when I completed my education I could enter the Order of the Sisters of Nevers, but like Pappy my sudden mysterious illness, towards the end of 1939, put all my hopes aside. I still believe that this was God's way of telling me that it was not to be. I accept and thank God still for changing the whole course of my life and vocation. Instead, my life has been spent working with and nursing every class of person, both in the hospitals and later in the community where I was privileged to serve and care for everyone from the cradle to the grave for twenty-five years.

So I accepted Pappy's proposal, and he bought me a neat sapphire and diamond engagement ring, which I still wear today with pride. During our nine months' engagement

CHAPTER SIX

period there were many ups and downs in our relationship. The most serious one, however, was because he thought that a wife should give up her profession and stay at home. I could never agree to having spent seven years studying to reach the top of my profession just to throw it all away. Also, neither of us was young, and we might never become parents. At that time, 1957, Pappy's wages were only nine pounds a week. True he had a semi-detached house, but he owed the building society one thousand pounds and was paying them back at the rate of eight pounds a month, with the result that there was nothing coming off the capital, only the interest they were charging.

On the ninth of August 1958, Pappy and I were married at the Church of the Most Blessed Sacrament, Braunstone, Leicester. It was a memorable day for me walking down the aisle in a flowing white gown with four bridesmaids. Pappy's grey suit had been made by the tailor Austin Reed of Leicester, with a lovely red paisley patterned tie. He was handsome on that day and I was very proud to be his bride. Pappy's brother and sister-in-law and their twelve-year-old daughter travelled from Ennis so Pappy's brother could be his best man, and my brother-in-law, John Kennedy, my sister Teresa's husband, gave me away.

We had the whole ceremony recorded, including the organ, choir, nuptial Mass, reception and apostolic blessing from Rome. We had this done specially for my aged mother in Ireland, who was unable to travel to Leicester. Two months later we found a recording company that made it into a long-playing record. Now thirty-three years later, I can sit in my lounge and relive that happy, memorable day all over again.

That same evening we travelled to Brighton and stayed at a small private hotel. That was my first time at that seaside. It was comfortable enough and clean, but foodwise it was inadequate for a man, with the result that we found ourselves going in and out of cafés for snacks. At that time Pappy weighed eleven stone, seven pounds, and though I say it, he looked a fine man and I was proud to be walking down the promenade with him. He loved fries and had no time for cold meals, always expecting bacon, eggs, sausage, or black pudding for his breakfast and tea.

One week later we returned home to our own house and Pappy changed his job from the retail trade to working in a mental hospital as a student male nurse. His wages dropped three pounds, so it was a case of me having to work to pay our way. Soon he was on nights and as he came home in the morning I would be preparing to leave for work. At times I felt strange and wondered how I was going to cope with Pappy's fussy food fads as well as holding down a demanding full-time job. He found the studying hard, and apart from anatomy and physiology I could not help him much because I never had any interest in mental illness, though I am sure the mental certificate would have helped me greatly in my job as a health visitor.

Six weeks after our return home we travelled to Ireland and took a large portable tape recorder so that my mother could listen to the whole wedding ceremony as if she had been present on the day. In fact, our house was filled with relatives, friends, and neighbours, as we held a mini reception all over again. They all loved it and many of the elderly people, including my dear mother, cried with joy.

During the part where Pappy and I made the promises to each other, Mother looked at me, saying, 'Is that you talking, Bridget?'

I replied, 'Yes, Mother, that's my voice.'

She cried more, but it was more from joy than sorrow. What a happy day that was!

7

Katrina, our first child, was conceived while we were in Ireland. I only had two periods after the wedding, so our time on our own was short-lived. Being a trained midwife, as soon as the first symptoms arrived I knew I was pregnant. My feelings were mixed, to say the least, and at that stage I would have given anything not to have been pregnant. Soon morning sickness commenced, and at times I felt so low I wondered if I could carry on with my demanding job as well as looking after a fussy husband foodwise and the upkeep of a three-bedroom house. I also worried in case there was anything wrong with my baby and I could not return to work. We needed the money badly because Pappy's wages as a student were abysmal.

After the first three months, I felt and slept better than I had ever done. I attended the local prenatal clinic, and apart from a low blood count I was fine. I carried on with my full-time job and gained very little weight, so I did not have to spend money on maternity clothes and the mothers did not even know I was having a baby. I carried on with my full-time health visiting job until eleven weeks before the birth. I was granted maternity leave provided I signed a form agreeing to return to work eight weeks after the birth. At this point it was a relief to be at home resting, because sometimes I felt exhausted at the end of the day.

During my waiting period I made a complete layette by hand of Viella material – 50 per cent wool and 50 per cent cotton. I made three long gowns, which the pattern stated would be suitable for the baby up to eighteen months. I made three simple underskirts that were suitable for a child up to one year. Many kind friends knitted vests and matinée coats that, together with two dozen towelling nappies and one dozen muslin nappies, completed the layette.

On sixteenth June, 1959, I had a show a few minutes after Pappy left for work. I rang the hospital and, being classed as an elderly primipara (mothers over thirty-five come into that category), I rang the taxi centre, which I had previously notified I might be calling on night or day. Pappy was colourblind, so there was no point in ringing him at that stage, as he could not drive me to the hospital, but later on that day I did ring to say I was in hospital.

As I was all right, I remained up all day, having castor oil and a hot bath (this was called a medical induction). At 10 o'clock that night they gave me a drug to help me sleep and relax, because by that time I was having a lot of labour pains. This drug made me very sick and resulted in severe vomiting; probably the castor oil, which was foul, did not help.

At 5.30 the next morning, I managed to deliver a beautiful baby daughter normally. She seemed perfect in every way and looked pink, with plenty of fair hair. The midwife who delivered her wrapped her in a warm blanket and put her to my breast. That to me was a wonderful moment and feeling, as she sucked straight away for a minute. The midwife took her away to be bathed, and I had a lovely cup of sweet tea, which to me tasted like manna from heaven. After the labour and vomiting, my mouth was parched and I could have drunk a potful. Soon after, I fell asleep for several hours, and I awoke refreshed and happy. That evening Pappy came straight from work and was ecstatic over our lovely baby daughter, whom we decided to call Katrina Maria, after Pappy's mother, who was call Catherine.

I stayed in hospital for ten days after the birth. Sadly, my milk supply did not increase, despite drinking pints of Lactogal, a substance to stimulate the breast glands to secrete more milk. During most feeds Katrina was test-weighed and she nearly always had to be supplemented with breast milk from the hospital bank.

The day I came home, Pappy came with a male friend

who was an usher at our wedding and a charge nurse at the same hospital as Pappy. When I entered the living room I saw this smart Slimline pram all made up and waiting for our Katrina. For a whole month I put her to my breast, but she nearly always needed a supplementary feed of breast milk, which the hospital ambulance delivered to my home daily. I used to thank God for such a wonderful service. It soon became apparent that my milk was not going to increase, and Katrina failed to gain sufficient weight at a month old.

Katrina was breast-fed for one month with the help of the bank milk, but her weight gain was insufficient and, sadly, I had to resort to Oster milk. Thank God she loved it and finally began to gain weight steadily, as well as sleeping better.

After eight weeks I returned to my full-time job as a health visitor and was fortunate in obtaining the services of a very nice, sensible lady who had brought up four children of her own and was now free to come to our house each day Monday to Friday and look after Katrina. I bathed and fed her before I left in the morning and was home again by 5 p.m. to nurse her and put her to bed. All the nanny had to do was see to Katrina at lunchtime and take her for a walk in the park and shops. As soon as Katrina was able to crawl she loved to pick daisies which the nanny used to make into daisy chains.

When Katrina was three years old we were able to get her into a local nursery school, which she loved. She stayed right through until 3 p.m. She had orange juice in the morning, a cooked lunch, and following an hour's lie-down she had milk and biscuits before she came home. She made rapid progress at school and was soon able to do some nice drawings. She loved the company of her little pals and did not want to come home when Nanny went to fetch her.

In 1962, I conceived my second child. Healthwise, the picture was very different this time. I did not feel well from day one. First, the morning sickness lasted all day and the very thought of cooking a meal in the evening was a nightmare. When I was only seven weeks pregnant I attended the local prenatal clinic at the same hospital as before, because instinctively I knew something was not right. I was examined by a senior gynaecologist who discovered I was going to miscarry. My womb was so retroverted (tilted) soon the foetus would have soon slipped out and probably I would not be able to have another child. He asked me to wait until he rang round the hospitals for the special ring to hold the baby in position until it was big enough to fill the cavity of the womb. It could be roughly five months before it was safe to remove the ring. Often I wished I did not have this extra worry. Every time I went to the toilet the ring came down and I had to put it back with toilet paper.

When I was four months pregnant Katrina developed mumps, and, as I had never had the infection as a child and was very low myself healthwise, ten days later I had all the symptoms of mumps, feeling grotty with swollen neck glands. I did not bother our doctor, but took it easy over the weekend and lay down when I could. By the Monday, however, I became very ill and could not keep even fluids down. By the time Pappy came home I had stiffness in my neck and a high fever. He called our doctor, who was also extremely worried and suggested we called a specialist from the infectious disease hospital. He came that same evening and after a thorough medical examination queried meningitis because of the vomiting, stiffness of the neck, high fever and impaired eyesight. At 9 o'clock the same night the ambulance came and took me and Pappy to Groby Road Hospital, Leicester. This hospital specialised in infectious diseases. On the way there I made a verbal will, telling Pappy what to do should I die. For instance, I made him promise to give some money to my aged mother who lived in Ireland. He laughed, saying, 'You are not going to die yet.' I felt so ill I could not care one way or the other.

On my arrival at the hospital, they put me in a single unit and gave me an injection, from which I fell asleep and did not waken until the following morning. I heard a baby cry, and even though my eyes were affected, I could see a baby standing up in a cot bed. For a moment in my hazy state I thought it was our Katrina and attempted to get out, but found I could not stand up. My head was pounding and the pain was excruciating.

CHAPTER SEVEN

Later on that morning the consultant came, saying they were going to perform a lumbar puncture. That means a large needle is inserted in between the fifth and sixth lumbar vertebras and fluid is removed from the spine to test its pressure. While I awaited this procedure, my parish priest came and heard my confession, sitting outside in the corridor. He gave me absolution. I found the procedure very distressing and for the rest of the day could not lift my head off the pillow.

The next day the consultant came to my room shortly after 8 a.m., saying the spinal fluid confirmed I was suffering from encephalitis lethargia, a serious complication of mumps, hence the high fever, stiffness of the neck, vomiting and partial sight loss. The treatment would last for ten days and involve three injections of a vaccine called gammaglobulin. I asked him how serious the condition was and how the baby inside me was going to live when I could not keep down food or fluids. He replied, 'You as a trained nurse and midwife should know that a growing baby will take all the stored nourishment which you collected and stored in the liver when you were well. To put it more bluntly, you will die before your baby.' I thought, *What a statement to make when I am so ill*, yet I knew what he said was right.

Following the ten days' gammaglobulin treatment I did not feel much better and I was too weak to stand up on my own, but the sickness and vomiting eased and I was able to keep down fluids and light food, though my temperature varied between normal and very high. As I lay there I thought about my little girl Katrina, who was being looked after by Barbara, my best friend. When the consultant next visited me I asked him whether I could go home and lie in bed there, have a paid home help and see my little girl? Also, it would help Pappy, who could not drive and was depending on kind neighbours to bring him to see me. The consultant was reasonable and said if my temperature remained stable I could go home the following Monday. I prayed it would come down and stay down. Thank God it did! Two weeks later, I came home as I went in, on a stretcher. I went in to my own bed, and it was like heaven after the hard hospital beds. That same afternoon, the home help organiser came to assess my needs. It was arranged that a home help would come each day from Monday to Friday and we paid the seven shillings and sixpence per hour for the service. She was a lovely lady who came at 8.30 a.m. took Katrina to nursery school, then came back and did some domestic work including small items of clothing that needed hand washing. Each day I began to regain some strength and drank lots of cups of oxo, but I still could not take tea or coffee and felt sickly most of the day.

Six weeks following my discharge we went for two weeks' holiday to Butlins holiday camp in Clacton-on-Sea. This holiday was booked previously by Pappy so I could have a complete rest, and Katrina was kept entertained with children of her own age by the Redcoats whom Butlins employed. Also we had chalet patrols in the evening making sure the children were safe and not crying. Day by day I regained my strength, and by the time the two weeks were up I felt almost well again. Two weeks after we came home, I returned to my job as a health visitor and I carried on with my life until eleven weeks before the baby was due to be born.

The next time I attended the prenatal clinic, however, my blood pressure was raised and the doctor warned me to rest as much as I could, otherwise I could have developed toxaemia of pregnancy. This is a condition where the blood pressure is raised, coupled with traces of protein in the urine as well as swelling of the ankles and fingers. So far I had no symptoms of that nature. Being a midwife myself, I knew how serious it was, so I rested as much as I could.

8

On the eleventh of November 1962, I was alone in the kitchen when a telegram arrived saying my mother had died in Ireland and her funeral was the next day. This was midday on a Monday, and I was alone. For a few minutes I froze, then I was devastated, and at that moment part of me died, too; yet in my heart I wanted to attend the funeral in Ireland. I asked God to help me, and he did. Straight away I got through to my Pappy and asked if he could come home immediately, as my mother had died. Then I rang the airport and managed to get a seat on a flight out that evening. When Pappy came home he implored me not to attempt it in my state of health, but my mind was made up. Our next-door neighbour said she would look after Katrina, and Pappy accompanied me when I drove to Birmingham Airport and he came home on the bus that evening. I touched down at Dublin at 8 o'clock that same night and had Jimmy, a former boyfriend of mine who had a hackney car, meet me and take me the fifty-six miles to my home. It was 9.30 p.m. when we arrived and met my sister Rose, who had been alone with my mother when she died. Rose was in a dazed state from the night before and said, 'Poor Bridie, our best friend in all the world is dead.'

As Rose was in a vague state, she did not or could not make me a cup of tea. Thankfully there was a nice Protestant neighbour who made me one. I remember her giving me an aspirin, because with the blood pressure being high and the stress of the journey my head was jumping with pain. Sadly, I did not see my darling mother, as she was lying before the high altar in our local chapel. In silence I wept bitterly when I reflected on my former happy homecomings when my dear mother used to meet me at the gate, putting her arms around me, saying, 'Thank God you're home safe. The kettle is boiling and your favourite is in the range oven.' In my extreme grief and exhaustion I lay in the same bed as Rose and fell into a deep sleep.

The next day, Tuesday, together with my grieving family, I attended the requiem Mass and burial of my mother and best friend in all the world. To be honest, that day I did not care whether I lived or died, yet when I thought of dear Pappy and little Katrina, as well as my as yet unborn baby, I knew I must soldier on for their sakes. That evening my brother Joe, God rest his soul, made me a lovely coddled egg with butter in a cup for my tea. He was always the one who looked after everyone, including my mother, who had pneumonia when I was seven. I remember seeing her lying in the settlebed in the kitchen. I remember, too, the priest giving her the last rites and coming over to me and putting his hand on my head.

Two days after Mother's funeral I returned to England and drove myself home from the airport. For the sake of Pappy and Katrina I tried to carry on normally, but deep down in my heart I knew that my life would never be the same again, because part of me died with my mother on the eleventh of November 1962. The night before she died, she had talked about me, saying if she died it would kill me and the baby. How right she was even in her dying state!

At the next clinic appointment after the funeral, the doctor was not at all pleased with the general state of my health. I told him that I had been to my mother's funeral in Ireland and I was not sleeping at night. He prescribed sodium amytal sleeping tablets, saying it was better to take a tablet and rest than walk about all night worrying about what might happen regarding something over which I had no control. I was even more worried now, because in my work I had known mothers who resorted to the drug thalidomide and had babies born deformed, some without limbs. I could have done with that drug myself but refrained in order to safeguard my baby.

CHAPTER EIGHT

That year, I longed to get Christmas over, because by then I was not feeling right in myself. At the same time, I tried my best to make it happy for Pappy's and Katrina's sake, and we did have a nice, peaceful, happy holiday together. On Saint Stephen's Day that year there was deep snow and black ice on the roads, and though we had been invited out, I was thanking God that because of weather conditions I could not drive the car, as I did not want to go out.

My next prenatal appointment was the twenty-eighth of December, also I had to see my gynaecologist, who told me in no uncertain terms that he was unhappy with both my blood pressure and my general state of health. At that stage, too, there were symptoms of mild toxaemia. He was quite stern and asked me to go straight home and make preparations for my little girl and be prepared to come in two days' time for complete rest and treatment until the baby was born. To be honest, I was not sorry, because at that stage I felt exhausted. He also told me to be prepared to be surgically induced should the blood pressure warrant it. (This term means they would have to start me in labour artificially by breaking the waters.) For five weeks I rarely woke up even when the matron came round. I was to all intents and purposes asleep most of the twenty-four hours.

On the twenty-second of January 1963, I was told by the ward sister that should I not go into labour normally that day I would have to be induced surgically. I was so weary at that stage I could no longer fight and agreed with the medical staff. Later that morning a priest came from Holy Cross Dominican Church and gave me Holy Communion. At 2 p.m. that day they induced me, and immediately I began having violent labour pains, one after another, so there was no time in between to relax. They did their best to ease the labour pains by injecting me.

At 6.45 p.m. I knew I was fully dilated and told the ward sister, who confirmed I was ready to commence pushing, so they wheeled me into the labour ward, where at 7.10 that evening I pushed my baby boy out into the cold, cold world and winter of 1963. The baby looked normal and had all his limbs, but he was filled with excess mucus and very, very drowsy and did not yell in the usual way. Straight away he was wrapped up and laid in a warm cot beside me. The sister recorded my blood pressure, which was very high. Normally, in toxaemia cases, blood pressure goes down as soon as the baby is born. Mine was so high that they had to keep me in the labour ward until 11 o'clock that night. Complicated with that was the fact that I could not see clearly, which suggested eclampsia, a kind of epileptic convulsion either before or after childbirth.

Eventually they took me back to my single room. Though they gave me a sedative I could not sleep. Also, my baby kept coughing and choking, and shakily I walked over to the cot and kept putting him on his side, fearing he might choke. The next day I felt as if the top of my head was leaving me, the pain was so intense. The sister took my blood pressure and immediately called my gynaecologist, who ordered morphia and hyasine to be given by injection. They took my baby to the nursery and put a notice on my door stating no visitors except my husband, and only for three minutes at a time. Even if I were able to sleep I was not allowed to, because every fifteen minutes there was either a nurse or a doctor taking my pulse and blood pressure.

One of the young doctors who came into my room at 1 am asked me what the time was.

I replied, 'Doctor, you have a watch on; you must know what the time is.'

He replied, 'Sorry, I was only testing your sight.'

That evening when Pappy came to visit me, he saw the notice on my door, which mentioned the drugs I was taking and naturally became very alarmed and called the sister in charge, saying, 'When I have a headache I get by on aspirins. Why is it necessary for my wife to be injected with hard drugs?'

She curtly replied, 'Mr Dunne, your wife has not been right from the moment of conception. You have not had a baby.'

Poor Pappy was speechless and very worried indeed. He kissed me goodnight and left to go home to a cold, empty house.

CHAPTER EIGHT

My baby was still in the nursery, and I will always maintain that removing him from me aggravated my already hypertensive state. I was injected with drugs to suppress lactation, so I never had the chance of letting my baby suckle at my breast, though I did not feel strong enough to attempt to feed him on the breast. By the fifth day my blood pressure lowered and I was allowed to have Mark John in my room and feed him with Ostermilk, which I had brought in with me. We had a priest come in and baptise him in the hospital, with the intention of having him done again later.

I came home with Mark John on the tenth day on a drug called Librium (ten milligrams strength) to try to lower the blood pressure. It did help to make me more stable, but every time I sat down I fell into a stupor of sleep. The day I brought Mark John home I dreaded him wakening up because I felt so ill and weak; also, I did not know how I was going to cope when Katrina came home from nursery school. At that stage, I felt I would never recover sufficiently to look after my two children and Pappy. Before I left the hospital I asked the top consultant why I became so ill following the birth. He said the reason was because I could not or did not cry when my darling mother died.

It took Mark John a whole month to wake up normally for his feeds, because he too had been drugged for a whole month, while in my womb, with the result that he was not gaining weight and I had to try to force the milk down him every three hours. However, after the month he woke up normally for his feeds and I fed him on demand. At about six weeks, he became a very handsome, happy, contented baby and was a joy to look after. I used to take him to my nearest child health centre to be weighed and examined. To me, considering the dicey pregnancy and the complications before and after, it was nothing short of a miracle he was normal.

When he was two months old, I went back to work as a health visitor, having obtained a nice, sensible nanny who came to my house to care for Mark John, give him his lunchtime feed, take him for a walk and fetch Katrina from the nursery school. Both children loved Nanna Hyman and

I was happy, too. I prepared all his feeds in advance as well as seeing to him morning and night.

9

When Mark John was three, there was no longer state nursery education provided, so unlike Katrina, we paid for him to attend a private nursery school. At first, he rebelled and showed his dislike by starting to wet the bed every night, though he had been toilet trained since the age of two. I thought at one stage that we would have to take him away. In sheer desperation, one night I told him he would have to go back to nappies again. He pleaded with me not to put a nappy on, saying he would not wet the bed any more. I did not and he never wet the bed again and settled down at the private nursery school.

When he was under five he went to a Catholic school, and on his first morning I dreaded leaving him, thinking he would rebel again. Instead, he went over to a toy motorcar and started playing with it as if he had always been there. I sat in my car outside for a while in tears. I need not have worried; he was happy. He stayed there until the age of eleven and during that time joined the cubs and scouts at the Catholic church. He became an altar boy, and I shall always look back with joy and happiness to the first time he served at a Mass for a wedding, when the groom gave him twenty-five pence. He rushed home, giving it to me. I put it in his money box. During those happy childhood years he became a footballer, joining a junior football team, and went to play in both Holland and Belgium with the club. While in Belgium, he scored a goal for his team. He was overjoyed and rang me that evening to tell me the news.

When he was eleven, he chose to go to a Catholic secondary state school and for a time made rapid progress in the subjects he liked, which were history and geography. He was weak in both English and maths, and by the age of fourteen hated the school and subjects, with the result that at the age of fifteen he transferred to another Catholic secondary school. He did not do very well there either, and it soon showed in his work. Looking back now, I am sure he was dyslexic and it was not discovered. I remember one open evening I attended, his class teacher said she thought in certain subjects he had brain blocks. He left school at the age of sixteen and started work in a factory specialising in Sheffield steel.

I often reflect in my quiet moments on how different things might have been for Mark John had he done what Pappy and I wanted him to do. He could have gone to a private school where the classes were smaller and perhaps could have found out why he was slow and failed to grasp certain subjects, but there is little use worrying about that now! At the age of eighteen he joined the army and trained to be a Coldstream Guard, where he made great progress and passed out with good results. I shall always remember attending the ceremony that day and seeing how handsome he looked in his Guards uniform. He had the world at his feet, having a choice where he wished to serve. He could have stayed in London at Horseguards Parade. Instead, he chose to be posted to Germany. This proved to be a mistake, as before long in his letters home he complained about the loneliness. In peacetime they were wound up like clockwork soldiers Monday to Friday. Saturday and Sunday they could smoke and drink themselves to death. No longer were they obliged to attend church each Sunday, only every three weeks. Before the year was up he broke down and had to come back home to mass unemployment in this country.

Katrina's education was somewhat different from Mark John's. At the age of five she went to a private convent school for a short period until a brand new Catholic state school was built in the same area. Most of the teachers, including the sisters transferred to the state Catholic school. This

CHAPTER NINE

meant that Katrina still had the same teachers, but unlike the small private school, this state Catholic school soon filled up to overflowing with Catholic children of all the surrounding areas of Leicester and County. Sadly, however, I soon noticed the quality of the education declined, with the result that my daughter, who sat the eleven plus at the age of ten, failed to get a place in a grammar school, which altered the whole course of her life.

At the age of eight Katrina developed quite a severe form of asthma, which meant she spent several weeks in hospital under skilled consultants. She was prescribed the drug Intal, which she inhaled through an inhaler. This was very effective in preventing an asthmatic attack. During that dreadful period, when all seemed black on the horizon, they carried out all the tests to find out the cause of this sudden asthma, and discovered the main cause was house dust and the living mites it contains. This was successfully treated by small weekly amounts of vaccine injected intradermally.

When Katrina was eleven and had to transfer to a secondary Catholic school, the nearest one was at least four miles away. This meant on cold wintry mornings she would have to catch two buses to get there. Pappy and I felt that would be cruel for a highly sensitive asthmatic child, so we were for a time in a real dilemma as what to do for the best. One evening, on my way home from work, I saw there was a small private secondary college within walking distance from our home. I went in and rang the bell, asking if it were possible to see the principal. It was, and soon I was telling her our problem over a cup of tea. She was a mother herself and understood, giving me a brochure to study.

When Pappy came home from work that evening I told him about the private day college within walking distance from our home. He was delighted. I called the college and made an appointment for all three of us to go the following morning. It was Pappy's day off, and we took Katrina as well. It was an answer to our prayers and problems, because it incorporated ballet and drama as well as all the academic subjects. Katrina had already been attending ballet classes privately, and at the age of seven, passed her first examination of the British Ballet Organisation. In fact, by the age of eleven she had already reached the elementary grade.

All three of us spent two hours at the college the next day, where Katrina sat the entrance examination and passed without any difficulty. It was an answer to all our prayers, and we were all happy at the outcome.

The following September, Katrina started her academic year at the college. She soon settled down and made many friends. She loved the smaller private classes, where you received almost individual attention. This could never happen in a state school, with thirty or more children with different levels of attainment. She still continued with Miss Mason's School of Dancing and Tap. Soon, however, she had to give that up and concentrate her whole attention on the Royal Academy of Dancing examinations.

Katrina's first Christmas at the college was a very happy one for us all. She played one of the ugly sisters with another student, and even that early she showed a distinct aptitude for drama, dance and singing. The next term we paid an extra eighteen pounds for her enrolment as a vocational student. This meant she had all her dancing and drama included in the education. She loved it and often spent the whole day there. Being a vocational student, she was entered for all the drama and dancing festivals in and around Leicester.

By the age of fifteen, she was an accomplished dancer and was included in a group that danced for and talked to Her Royal Highness Princess Anne at the Grand Hotel Leicester in 1974, the proceeds of which went to the Save the Children Fund, of which Her Royal Highness Princess Anne is patron. Shortly after that, Katrina, with the same group, in ballroom gowns, danced at Belvoir Castle, the home of the Duke and Duchess of Rutland.

That same year Katrina sat and passed three Oxford O levels, in art, English and religious education. At the age of sixteen, she sat and passed all the Royal Academy of Dancing examinations, as well as gaining gold medals in London for both stage and ballroom dancing.

When she was just seventeen, she won a scholarship to the famous Arts Educational School, Golden Lane, London, where she studied dancing and drama for three years. During her second term there, we paid extra for her to have professional singing lessons on the advice of her singing teacher. This proved very helpful later when Katrina attended auditions for jobs. Before she was twenty-one, she received her precious Equity card and a five-months' contract in Cairo, Egypt. While there, she rode camels in the Arabian desert and visited all the famous places and tombs. While there, she did, however, become very homesick for England and, sadly, for the first time in her life she started to smoke. She has since tried hard so many times to give it up, to no avail.

Her next assignments were Germany and Athens, where she spent three years. During the time she worked there, she studied languages and became fluent in German, Greek and French. This is a great asset, especially now as we approach 1992.

Five years ago Katrina returned to London, and she now lives in Kensington. Like many other actresses, she has no work, but that does not deter her. Instead, she works as a freelance interpreter for foreign delegations visiting the country. Often she meets them at the airport and arranges cabs to take them to the famous London hotels, where she has dinner with them. In this job she gets contracts all over England, as well as Paris, Glasgow, Dublin and Cork, with all expenses paid.

Two years ago on my birthday, I had a phone call from her telling me she was coming to the Grand Hotel in Leicester for four nights with a German delegation. During her time here she invited me to join her for a birthday dinner at the Grand. It was such a happy occasion, and I was so proud of her.

Finally, I am eternally grateful to the private college where she was educated, especially considering the asthma and the poor state of her health at the age of seven. The training she received during those formative years prepared her to meet people and walk happily in any circle. Neither Pappy nor I regretted one penny of the cost, and I would be prepared to do it all over again if we had to. I am positive that Katrina would never have succeeded in the same way in a state school.

10

On the twenty-eighth of June 1974, Pappy, having gone to bed as usual the night before, had a brain stroke in the night. The first thing I noticed the next morning was that he could not hold a cup of tea in his hand because of a severe trembling. The tea was all over the sheets. This frightened the life out of Katrina, who was only fifteen at the time and always brought us a cup of tea on Pappy's day off. I reassured her, saying, 'Do not worry, Katrina, I shall see to him.' Hearing that she ran out of the room. Then I went over to Pappy, asking him what was wrong. He could not answer me because his speech was severely impaired. I knew then it was a brain stroke, because since 1968 he had been on medication for high blood pressure.

I dressed and came down, stressing he should stay in bed and I would bring his breakfast up. He indicated he would like to come down, and I insisted he did not attempt to come down on his own. I returned quickly, to find him in a standing position clutching his chest of drawers with both hands. I helped him back into bed and gave him some tea and thin porridge, so it would be easy to swallow. I then helped him to the toilet and found his motions were watery. This is quite common following a sudden stroke. I washed him and put clean pyjamas on and helped him back to bed.

I rang our doctor and relayed his symptoms; he said he would call after surgery that morning. Meantime, I had some breakfast and rang the health department saying what had happened and I would not be in that day. They were very helpful, asking if I needed any help. I thanked them, saying I could manage.

Less than an hour later, I went back to see how Pappy was and was shocked to find he was doubly incontinent. I washed and changed him again, just putting pyjama top on. I found a plastic sheet that I had for the children and changed the bottom sheet, rolling him from side to side as best I could.

Later on that day, the doctor came and, having examined Pappy thoroughly including his reflexes, stated he had not suffered a stroke. He agreed he was very ill and gave me a prescription for antibiotics and said he would be back on Monday. Naturally, I did not believe him! I knew only too well Pappy had suffered a stroke, albeit it not a major one, otherwise how could one account for a man who came home from work the evening before, had his meal and watched television and went to bed at the normal time, then the next morning could not hold a cup of tea in his hand or speak and had a haemiplegia down the right side as well as having lost control of his bodily functions? The doctor did, however, offer to send a male nurse in to wash and change him. I thanked him and declined. I shall always remember that evening; when Mark John came home from school I was sponging the carpet in the bedroom and there was a smell. He ran out of the room crying. Who could blame him or how could he be expected to understand what had happened to his daddy overnight?

That weekend was black and dreadful for me; I was on my own, as Katrina was on one of her dancing engagements in Leeds. She did not want to get in the coach that was driving them there, but I insisted she go. All weekend I kept Pappy warm and comfortable, as well as giving him his antibiotics and nourishing drinks all through the night. The good nursing paid dividends, because the next day there was a slight improvement in his movements and speech, also there was some control of his bladder and bowels. I told him that should the improvement continue I would get him up on Sunday for a short while and sit him out in his chair. His speech was clearer, and he asked me could he have his lovely black suit on? Pappy loved smart, expensive clothes, and of

CHAPTER TEN

all his suits he loved the black one best! I said yes. Meantime, the canon from St Thomas Church brought him Holy Communion.

At 1 p.m. on the Monday, our doctor came back and I had Pappy fully dressed, sitting in his chair in the bedroom.

The doctor was quite taken aback when he saw Pappy, saying, 'Mrs Dunne, you are wonderful. How did you do so much in such a short time? You must have had a dreadful weekend.'

I said, 'I did.'

He suggested that in a day or two Pappy could come downstairs.

The following Friday, he was so much better I drove him one hundred miles to a lovely little seaside resort that he loved. These few days had been booked previously, and I had informed the landlady in advance about Pappy's illness, asking if we could book in on a daily basis, so if his condition changed I could return home. She agreed. He was all right for the first two days, but begged me to bring him home the next day. I said of course I would. I explained to our landlady, and she was quite happy with the arrangements. On the way back, I had to stop several times so he could empty his bladder. He was on medication for high blood pressure and was taking very strong diuretics: *water tablets*. I always carried a small chamber pot in the car, which he could use without leaving the seat. This was invaluable for cases like Pappy. Slowly he improved beyond measure, and in about six weeks he got full use of his arm and as well full control of both bladder and bowels.

In September that year his firm allowed him to return to a light office job. We were all delighted, because I knew only too well that he would have hated not to be fully independent. At night towards the end of November he frequently complained of indigestion, which was relieved at first with an antacid mixture and milk of magnesia tablets.

On the eleventh of November that year, he had an appointment with his optician at 9.30 a.m. I arranged to drop him there on my way to work. I noticed, however, that he was slower both in his movements and memory. With that, together with his constant indigestion symptoms, I feared the worst, so like many other occasions I went to work with a heavy heart.

It was Friday evening and I arrived home at 4.30, put my car in the garage and ran up the back garden into the house. As I opened the back door I shouted 'Pappy, how did you get on?' I then noticed his lunch uneaten on the table. With that I ran straight into the hall, and to my horror I heard a groan coming from the landing. I bolted up the stairs, and there, lying on the bathroom floor, was my Pappy. I shall never forget the look on his ashen grey face and the huge beads of sweat pouring down his cheeks. As a nurse I knew death was only minutes away. I briefly spoke and he tried to indicate it was his chest. Immediately I rang the 999 service, saying it was a massive heart attack. In less than ten minutes the ambulance arrived with all the latest medical equipment for resuscitation, which the trained medic started on the spot. As the ambulance with police escort was leaving, I saw Mark John walk down the road from school. Being a child, he asked me had I done his egg and chips. I said, 'No, I will do that when I come home. There are sandwiches on the table.'

On arrival at the hospital Pappy was admitted straight to the intensive care unit in the cardiac section and attached to a heart monitor. As soon as the consultant saw him he ordered an injection of diamorphine, after which Pappy became very distressed and violent. Both the consultant and I realised that this was probably due to anoxia (lack of oxygen to the brain), which meant some vital part of his brain was damaged. They had to hold him down on the bed and give him a second injection in order that he could be examined. Ten minutes later, as I stood by his bed on that cold, bitter November night holding his hand, it was the blackest night of my life. Suddenly the hand I was holding flopped down. I thought Pappy had died at that moment. Instead, he fell into a comatose sleep. It was 7 p.m. and at that stage I thought it was best for me to get home to my children and ring our parish priest to visit and give Pappy the last rites of the Roman Catholic Church.

As I had no car, I came out of the hospital and stood in

CHAPTER TEN

the bitter cold waiting for a bus that never seemed to come. I was brain numb with the shock, as well as cold and hungry, as I had not eaten since the morning. When I finally arrived home, Katrina was there to greet me, putting her arms around me, saying, 'Mummy, come in to the fire. I have your egg, beans, and chips ready. It's in the oven.' At that critical moment it was a great comfort and joy for me to have two lovely children. I asked where Mark John was. She replied, 'He went to the scout meeting.' In a way I was glad he did! I was so shocked and shaky I just threw myself in front of the fire and had a cup of tea with a teaspoonful of brandy in it.

At 10.30 p.m., mentally and physically exhausted, I tumbled into a warm bed, and soon I fell into a heavy sleep, not knowing when the phone would ring to say my Pappy had died. At 4 a.m. I woke up in a stupor and felt the cold body of my late mother trying to get out of bed. My immediate thoughts were that Pappy had died beside me! I thought any minute now my phone would ring to ask me to come to the hospital; it did not.

The next day was Saturday and both my children were at home with me. I rang the hospital at 8 a.m. to ask how Pappy was. I spoke to the ward sister, who said he had improved dramatically and had a peaceful night. I thanked God from the bottom of my heart. In the afternoon, all three of us went to visit Pappy and found the Reverend Ireson, Katrina's college headmaster, there. He was delighted, saying, 'Now, Mr Dunne, you have all your loving family around you; you will soon be well again.' Gradually, that did happen, because when we visited him on the Sunday, Pappy was moved out of intensive care and was sitting in a chair in the main ward. Physically there was a marked improvement, but mentally he was very forgetful and confused. Both my children noticed it and wanted to come away as soon as possible. Who could blame them? How could they understand what happened to the daddy they knew both before the brain stroke and the heart attack? The brain stroke took ten years from Pappy's life straight away. With the heart attack that followed his heart muscles were permanently damaged, and he would be an invalid, living only under constant medication, which had side effects.

On the twelfth day Pappy was discharged, still very confused, but glad to be home. The day he came home I had grave doubts as to how I, with two children and a demanding full-time job, could carry on as before, because it would mean leaving Pappy alone in the house during the day. I used to leave his lunch ready on the kitchen table, also his medication, and a kind neighbour used to pop in and make sure he had his tablets, but because of the nature of his illness, I could soon sense they would rather not. There was one person, however, my friend Sheila with whom I trained, who always came in and had a chat with Pappy and brought magazines for him to read. Thankfully, with all the drugs he was on he slept most of the day.

Christmas 1974 neither I nor my children will ever forget, as Pappy was quite mental and deranged. For instance, on Christmas Eve morning he accused our friendly postman of having a mad dog with him when he delivered our Christmas mail. I had to run after the postman and tell him about Pappy's illness and not to take any offence. Both my children were scared, and apart from Christmas dinner, they spent most of the day in their bedrooms. It was so bad, we never even opened a card or letter and all the children's parcels were left unopened by the Christmas tree. That year, I had a present of a long playing record of John Hanson that disappeared and was not found for two months. At 3 a.m. on the Feast of Saint Stephen, I awoke to find Pappy standing over me in the bed, saying, 'The house is packed with policemen.' I had to get up, make a drink and coax him back to bed.

The next day I was desperate for expert medical help, so I sent for our doctor, who visited as soon as he could. He saw how things were and called in a consultant psychiatrist from the local hospital. He came that same day at 5 p.m. He was a rather abrupt man who did not mince his words and did not seem to understand what the real problem was. He examined Pappy thoroughly and asked all the relevant questions, then asked Pappy a lot of current-event type questions such as who was the prime minister of England and who was the present queen. Pappy became rather annoyed because even he in his present state did not want to know. As the doctor left, not having helped me in any way, I told him I had a demanding full-time job as well as two school children to be considered. He came back and produced a large Largactil tablet, which I was to give Pappy with a milk drink that night. He did not even offer to have Pappy admitted to hospital for a few days for tests, and because I was a nurse, no one could help me in any way. At that moment, I would have given everything I possessed for positive help and guidance. I had to accept that Pappy would never recover and would need constant care and attention for the rest of his life. The drug (Largactil) caused severe side effects. For instance, he developed symptoms of Parkinson's disease, full of shakes and tremors, which caused him difficulty in feeding himself. I told our doctor, and he suggested we stop the drug altogether. This I did, and there was a marked improvement and the tremors finally stopped.

In 1979, Pappy expressed a longing to visit his home town Ennis. Because he so longed to go, I arranged the trip, having a taxi from our door to Birmingham Airport and a plane from Birmingham to Dublin, then another plane from Dublin to Shannon. I also arranged for Pappy to be wheeled inside by a porter, because by that time he used to become very breathless on exertion and could not walk up and down steps. It was late March and still bitterly cold, with east winds. I had previously arranged our accommodation in Ennis, and a taxi from Shannon to take us the seventeen miles from the airport to the town. I carried all his medication in my handbag.

When we finally arrived at our guest house it was midnight and bitterly cold. I put my bag down to ring the bell of the house where we were staying. In that moment Pappy seemed to be collapsing on the street. I managed to help him by leaning him over the bonnet of a car that was parked outside the door. When the landlady opened the door she was deeply shocked because Pappy looked like death and was unaware of what was happening. We both virtually carried him inside to the warm room, where there was a lovely coal fire in an open grate. We sat Pappy down and undid his clothes, and I fed him with a cup of sweet tea. He came round and asked us what had happened; he did not remember a thing. Later, after a good rest, we had another pot of tea and a soft-boiled egg with toast. As soon as he was well enough I took him to bed and I went to bed myself, and thankfully we both had a good night.

In the morning, which was Friday, following breakfast we walked slowly to the lovely cathedral in Ennis, where Pappy had made his First Holy Communion and confirmation many years before. He still had vivid memories of those happy days. At the cathedral, he met many old friends that he used to know both as an altar boy and in the guild of Saint Francis of Assisi. We went into a café and had a hot cup of coffee, after which I took him to visit a friend of his who worked in a bank. He greeted Pappy with open arms, saying, 'A hundred thousand welcomes, Pappy,' in Gaelic: *Caed mile failte*. Our next stop was at a lovely warm Irish public house for lunch, and poor Pappy, who was weary by then, made straight for a seat by the warm coal and log fire.

At 6 p.m. we walked slowly back towards our guest house, and as we came close to the cathedral the Angelus bell was ringing and both of us stopped to recite the Angelus. Just a few minutes later, the bell was ringing to receive the funeral of a native, for which Pappy removed his hat and blessed himself with tears in his eyes. In his poor state of health at that moment I could vividly imagine what his innermost thoughts were. He did not speak.

That night and early Saturday morning, Pappy became very, very ill. I took his pulse, and he seemed to be in heart block, when his pulse rate was just about fifty beats per minute. I had to call the landlady and ask if I could have a doctor immediately. She was so understanding and rang her own doctor, who arrived in less than fifteen minutes still in his pyjamas. He was a pleasant young doctor who had all the medical expertise and equipment with him, including a portable machine for recording the heart's state. He tried the pulse beat in the various parts of the body and came to the same conclusion as I did – Pappy was in heart block. This

CHAPTER TEN

would mean his immediate admission to the hospital in Ennis. Less than ten minutes later the ambulance came, accompanied by a trained nurse and all the lifesaving equipment for the short journey. I went with Pappy and tried to keep him talking as well as comforting him.

On arrival at the hospital, Pappy was examined by a top cardiologist from the States, who was spending some time at that hospital and had a lot of knowledge of pacemakers to help the already worn heart. Following emergency treatment by injection in the reception Pappy was admitted to the cardiac unit. Here, like the Leicester hospital in 1974, he became very agitated and abusive. Soon, however, like Leicester, the injection took effect and he fell into a comatose sleep, almost likened to unconsciousness. This continued for the next three days. Each day I raced backwards and forwards to the hospital, staying for about two hours at a time, holding his hand and talking to him, but there was no response. I was fully convinced that that was it; Pappy had come home to die in his native Ennis. On the Sunday night I sent word to his nieces who lived in the town. They went straight to his bedside, spending one hour there talking about old times in Ennis; still he did not respond. They came back to my guest house, and I was very glad to have some support. They took me out to a hotel for a drink and a bite to eat. At that time, too, there was both a postal and telephone strike in the Irish Republic, and I was unable to contact my kind friends who were looking after my son Mark John, who was still at school and was expecting me home on the Wednesday.

The day before my return I went to the hospital to see Pappy and the cardiologist, who on Pappy's admission thought maybe they could fit a pacemaker to help his worn and tired heart. However, he told me that owing to Pappy's poor condition, they had decided not to carry out the small operation. Needless to say, I was sorely disappointed, but there was nothing I could do, only accept the advice of the expert. Pappy gradually came round, but was still too ill for the journey by ambulance back to Leicester. With a heavy heart I had to return to my son and job in Leicester.

Ten days later, Pappy came by air and ambulance to

Birmingham Airport, where I met him and the trained nurse who had looked after him on the journey. She gave me all his case notes for our doctor. I was shocked, however, when I saw Pappy had a bag filled with urine strapped to his leg. He looked years older and was in a pretty poor state. Thankfully, when I arrived home my daughter, Katrina, came out to meet us and helped us in with her father, who was overjoyed to see her; so was I! Poor Pappy was smiling and happy again to be in his own home. Soon I made a pot of tea and his favourite – boiled egg – which he ate with relish. I took him to his bedroom, emptied his very full bag of urine, gave him his tablets and put him to bed. Before I left the room he was fast asleep.

When the weather was fine I used to sit Pappy out on our patio, where he listened to and watched all the various garden birds. He recovered sufficiently for me to take him to Mass every Sunday, and when the weekends were reasonable I took him out for a ride and picnic. He loved the car and never failed to tell me how grateful he was for everything I did for him. During that eight years, many times I thought I would lose my senses and felt like walking out and never returning. I thank God I stayed.

About the third of February 1982, during the night Pappy complained of a severe stabbing pain in his right side, which seemed to radiate from back to front. The following morning, he was deeply jaundiced from his eyes to his toes. I sent for the doctor, who referred Pappy to the hospital for immediate admission. He was admitted to the surgical ward, and they carried out all the tests and X rays to try and find out what the problem was. When I went back that first evening to see Pappy, the doctor told me he thought Pappy had cancer of the pancreas, but that the diagnosis was not positive at this stage. The next day was Thursday and they gave Pappy a light anaesthetic before taking him down to the theatre, where they put a fishnet with a light down his trachea and oesophagus and into the stomach, where they found the common bile duct packed with stones. They tried to dislodge them but were unsuccessful. That evening, when I arrived to visit Pappy, the porter was wheeling him into the ward and

CHAPTER TEN

Pappy was in a very distressful state, shouting abuse at everyone, including me. However, after a while he fell asleep and I left to come home. The next day when I went to see him there was a consultant with a group of doctors round Pappy's bed. I waited outside until they finished. Then the surgeon, whom I knew, told Pappy and me that unless he was operated on soon, the pancreas would fill with pus and he would die a slow, painful death. So we were faced with Hobson's choice. Pappy chose surgery, and because he felt something was being done for him he was delighted. He sat up in the bed and signed the anaesthetic form in his beautiful copperplate handwriting. I shuddered at the thought that in the circumstances I could never have signed that form. For one thing, I did not think his heart would stand the general anaesthetic.

The next day was Friday, and Pappy was to have a major operation to remove his gallbladder. This surgery is far more complicated in the male, as the stomach has to be moved to get there. The doctor told me the night before not to ring until 7 p.m. because Pappy would be admitted straight to the intensive care unit from the theatre. I did not ring until 7.30 p.m. when they told me his condition was fair and he was still asleep.

The next day Katrina was coming home from Germany especially to see her father. I had arranged to meet her and go straight to the hospital. In case she had nothing to eat I packed a flask of coffee and sandwiches which she could eat in the car. At the hospital we went to the nurses' station and were told Pappy was in the main ward and out of intensive care. I could hardly believe it. The nurse did say he would be too sedated to talk much, but he did speak and was delighted to see Katrina. Before we left, however, he complained of a pain in his chest. I informed sister on the way out what he said. She replied, 'Do not worry, Mrs Dunne. He is too sedated to know.' I had my own thoughts about that, but we left and came home.

Sunday morning, about 7 o'clock they called me to the hospital saying Pappy had a severe heart attack in the night and had been moved back into intensive care. I had a quick cup of coffee, told Katrina the news and left for the hospital. I spent the whole day there, because he was very poorly indeed, but he was receiving expert care and attention. The next day we all went to visit him and he asked for the priest to visit him. I rang from the hospital, and the priest came while we were there and gave Pappy the last rites again.

By the next Monday I went to visit him in the morning and was delighted to find him sitting out in a chair reading the morning newspaper, which he told me to take home when he had finished reading it. The doctor came round when I was there and told the nurse Pappy's stitches could come out and he could start eating light food from that day. At that, Pappy's face lit up. He was so much better we even discussed him going down to Norfolk to convalesce when he came out. I went home elated.

But the next day when I visited him things were not so rosy. Pappy had developed pneumonia symptoms, for which they were treating him with strong antibiotics. I did not like the look of him, and he was so ill he hardly spoke all the time I was there. I came home heavy-hearted, hoping the treatment would work. The next day when I went, as soon as I came through the door I could see Pappy's bed going up and down; then the nurse came and said the doctor wanted to speak to me. I could see why, but did not understand how all this had come about so soon. The doctor told me Pappy had developed a raging pneumonia and that unless he responded to treatment he would not live more than twenty-four hours. I did not think in his state he could live that long. On my way home that night I took the number of the funeral undertaker, whom I was having to do Pappy's funeral should he die.

The next day there was a slight improvement in his condition. I spent most of the day at his bedside mopping his brow and trying to get some fluids down him. That afternoon, our priest came, and as we sat with Pappy he looked at me and pleaded with me to take him home. I promised I would as soon as possible, but with all the tubes he had in I could not look after him alone. I would need another nurse all the time. I felt bad having to leave him there, but what could I do in the circumstances? I was pleased that Pappy understood, because he said, 'I know you will, darling.' He lingered on for two more weeks, but his chest never cleared despite constant physiotherapy. On Saturday morning, twentieth March 1982, the hospital sent for me at 7 o'clock, saying Pappy had deteriorated in the night and they feared his lung had spontaneously collapsed and unless they could reinflate it he could not live. I pleaded with the consultant not to intervene further, because Pappy was dying. He replied, 'Mrs Dunne, you are a trained nurse and would do everything in your power to save life. If we do not try, we will regret it. However, if we try and fail, we will have no regrets.'

At that moment the hospital chaplain came to read all the prayers for the dying and gave Pappy Holy Communion behind the screens. The priest looked at me and said, 'Do not worry, Mrs Dunne. Your husband is so happy.' As the priest left, he laid his hand on Pappy's forehead and blessed him.

At that, Pappy lifted his right hand and said, 'Goodbye, Father, and God bless you.'

That afternoon, they did reinflate Pappy's collapsed lung, and when I left at 6 o'clock that evening, I said to him that I had better go home and have something to eat, to which he replied, 'Yes, Bridie, you go home and see about your bungalow.' They were his last words to me.

On Sunday, the twenty-first of March 1982, one door shut firmly on my life. As I sat by my husband's bed, with his hand firmly locked in mine, he died. At that moment, twenty-five years of our sharing and caring life together flashed before my eyes and I was alone. I shall never forget that day. It was Mothering Sunday, and our front garden was ablaze with daffodils and narcissi. On my way to the hospital that Sunday, I said to myself, 'Why not make this 'Fathering Sunday?' However, as soon as I reached the door of Pappy's room, being a trained nurse, I knew instinctively that the end of the chapter was only hours away. He was unconscious. The nurse that was attending him said he became unconscious at noon. All the while there was a small tear falling on his left cheek, which I kept gently wiping away. I was delighted, however, when the nurse told me he was fully conscious and with our priest had recited all the prayers for the dying clearly.

At 4 p.m. that day, Pappy died just as peacefully as a child falling asleep in his mother's arms. I firmly believe that after so much suffering he too fell asleep in the comforting arms of Jesus! As a nurse, I had stood by hundreds of patients dying, but Pappy died as he lived, in the firm faith of meeting Jesus face to face.

One hour later, it was comforting for me to help the nurse to wash and lay out my beloved husband in the brown shroud of Saint Francis of Assisi, whom he had always loved in life. As I kissed him a last goodbye I laid a white narcissus from our garden entwined in his rosary beads on his chest. He looked so happy lying there that even I in my lonely state would never have wished him to wake and suffer further.

That Sunday night as I sat alone in our bungalow, pondering what my future held in store for me, the bell rang and I was delighted to see our little priest, who for the six weeks previously I had met at the hospital bedside of Pappy. In fact, it was Father Brendan who was with me the day that Pappy asked me to bring him home. Sadly, that did not happen, but the night Pappy was received into the church I had his coffin brought into our kitchen, where all the family bade our last farewells, thus keeping my promise. Pappy would have liked that!

On Tuesday before Pappy's funeral, God opened another door on my life. It was a nursing officer asking me back to do a part-time health visitor's job. (I had retired from my full-time job in 1979). She was not aware of my bereavement and apologised profusely when she heard. I told her not to worry and arranged to come and see her the following week, and almost straight away I went back to do a part-time health visiting job. For me, it was a lifesaver. Otherwise, I might have gone on Valium, which my doctor advised, but I had resisted. I am glad I did! Finally, for anyone in my position, I would just say a job that you are happy in is the finest tranquilliser you could ever have.

11

One year after Pappy's death I arranged with the stonemason to have a simple white marble stone erected on his grave at Wigston cemetery with a simple inscription which read as follows: 'In loving memory of a devoted husband and loving father.' His grave occupies a lovely sunny spot shadowed by four pretty yew.trees which are a delight to me every time I visit there. I keep a bouquet of colourful silk flowers on his grave all the year round. Three times a year I change them to match the flowers in season. I am glad he was buried not cremated, because, to me, a Catholic, cremation seems so final. A grave and stone is so comforting to visit, meditate and pray there, and even when I am at my lowest ebb I derive great satisfaction from a visit to Pappy's grave. Incidentally, I shall be buried there as well.

In June 1983, my only son Mark decided to marry his girlfriend Louise in a register office in Huddersfield. They were both twenty years old, immature and had no idea of the commitment of marriage. To me, as a devout Roman Catholic, I was broken-hearted that my son was marrying in a register office which according to the teachings of Rome is not a marriage at all. Louise was a Methodist who long since ceased to practise. Both her parents and I pleaded with them to wait but they would not listen. Against my conscience I agreed that it was my duty to attend the ceremony, also my sister and her husband came from Liverpool to support Mark. It was a most beautiful summer's day, June 18th, and they looked a delightful happy young couple. Her parents made the most of it and gave us a wonderful day and a sumptuous reception, including a buffet at night which went on right into the early morning. The cost was £1000, when costs were more reasonable then than they are now. At the back of my mind I could not help thinking what a waste of money when they were living in a poky damp room in Huddersfield and had no money and were having to borrow. Still, that's what Louise wanted and she was an only daughter and liked to have her own way.

In 1984, they had a baby girl whom they called Hazel Zena. By that time they were given an old council house in Leicester. It was bare and cold; I paid for the whole house to be carpeted. I also bought lots of things for the baby such as a clothes horse for the nappies and a nursery fireguard. Her parents bought her a washing machine. Louise was an excellent little mother who despite poor conditions breast-fed Hazel satisfactorily. Hazel was an intelligent child who by the age of eighteen months could speak fluently. They used to visit me three and four times a week, when Hazel used to make straight for the biscuit tin.

Just two years to the day of the fairytale wedding Louise's relatives came and took her and Hazel as well as most of their wedding presents back to Huddersfield. She never discussed it with me on her frequent visits here. She apparently told Mark she loved him but could not live with him – some love!

Mark was quite devastated when he broke the news to me. In fact, he was quite mental, and I could understand it being left alone in a near empty council house bereft of his wife and child. What a waste of a young life. Several times after she left he hitchhiked to Huddersfield to see Louise and Hazel. I remember one cold night particularly, I was on my way home from work and I could see Mark walking in Saffron Lane eating a few chips having been to Huddersfield. He looked so weary and dejected, it broke my heart. I took him home with me, made him a meal. After eating he had a hot bath and changed his clothes. That night in bed as I said my prayers and cried myself to sleep I thought how evil divorce is and how it destroys the children and the partner who is left.

CHAPTER ELEVEN

Many times during that year Mark was near to suicide and one particular night rang me at 1 am, saying 'I love you' and that he was going to kill himself. I pleaded with him to tell me where he was and I would come and fetch him home. It was a cry for help. I got dressed, picked him up and brought him back; that night if had I not been at home to listen I could have lost my son for ever.

Two years later Louise filed for divorce and Mark was in no position to contest it so the divorce was granted with the condition that she could not change Hazel's name until she either married or reached the age of twenty-one years old. Though I had been sending cards and presents to the child the last time I heard from Louise was when she needed to know if Mark was still living in the council house which they shared until she walked out with Hazel two years before. Every year since I have pleaded with Louise for snaps and news of Hazel but she never replies. I am sure,however, that Hazel, now eleven years old, will want to know who her father and paternal grandmaare, also I hope and pray that one day she will walk through my door and say, 'Hello grandma'.

In 1985, I started writing seriously, mainly short factual articles in relation to my own life experiences in medicine of which I had a vast knowledge. My first acceptance was in *Nursery World* on the dangers of the use of electric blankets in young children's cots and beds. This was from my own experience with my own daughter when she was two years old. My husband who always put Kathleen to bed forgot to turn off the blanket when he took her to bed. Thank God, we always went up to see her about 9 p.m. and, to our dismay found little Kathleen whimpering on top of the bed. For that article I received the princely sum of £3. Naturally, I was delighted. I knew then that my forte was in fact, sad medical articles. That year I made quite a small income on writing medical articles for the *Nursing Mirror, Nursing Times* and *Pulse*. Following my success with nursing journals I wrote two short stories and they too, were accepted, by *The Irish Messenger of the Sacred Heart* and a magazine called *Catholic Fireside*. My greatest thrill, however, was an article on Euthanasia which was published by the *Sunday Times*.

In 1987 I wrote a short story about my own life and sent it to a professional magazine whose editor suggested that I should think seriously about writing a book and make this story the first chapter. I gave it great thought during many sleepless nights and decided to carry on by going back to my childhood in Ireland, then onto my schooldays both in Ireland and Britain. Lastly, I wrote about my professional life, my marriage in 1959, my two children, their childhood education and careers. My final chapter related to my late husband's illness and death in 1992. Even today, twelve years on; I am convinced it was the greatest challenge of my professional life when, for eight years, I saw this man fade away both physically and mentally and I was unable to make him well again. However, I will always thank God for my being with him when he was dying even if it was only to keep wiping away a single tear from his cheek.

In July 1993, my daughter Katrina gave me a lovely grandson called Maximilian and he has been a sheer delight for me to savour. At Katrina's request he was baptised here at St Mary's church Wigston on Sunday 27th November. This joy is more than I could ever have wished for and I did all in my power to make it a very wonderful occasion.